Will
the Defense
Please
Rest?

Will the Defense Please Rest?

A Guide to Marital Harmony

Les Carter

BAKER BOOK HOUSE
Grand Rapids, Michigan 49506

Contents

Introduction

Dick and Lisa sat in my office, obviously feeling awkward and uncomfortable about seeing a counselor. The tension in the room was thick.

"We want our marriage to work," Dick explained. "We've been together too long to just throw our relationship away. Besides, we don't believe in divorce."

At this point, Lisa threw in a bit of sarcasm. "You can say you don't believe in divorce now, but that sure isn't what you were saying to me last week."

I could tell this aggravated Dick. It was not what he had expected Lisa to say. "Oh, come on," he retorted. "Don't you know that everyone says things they don't really mean? Besides, you've been known to say a few hateful things to me. Or don't you remember?"

"Here we go again!" was Lisa's reply. "I thought we could come in here and learn to talk things out in a sane way. But I don't know if there's any help for us."

Dick looked at me exasperatedly. "Whenever we try to discuss our marriage, it always starts this way." Then, looking to Lisa, he asked, "Do you want to try or don't you?"

"Why are you trying to put the monkey on my back?" Lisa shot back. "What about you? Do you want to try?"

With this, Dick fell silent. His eyes darted to the floor and a sulking look crept over his face. I had an intuitive suspicion that he frequently used this "quiet tactic" when discussions didn't go as he desired. Lisa, on the other hand, had a fiery look in her eyes. She seemed ready to "slug it out" with her husband.

Within a few minutes a wall of defensiveness had been erected right there in my office. This couple didn't have to explain to me why they were seeking marriage counseling. They were illustrating their problems quite clearly. Listening to them, I wanted to jump into the conversation and say: "Will the defense please rest!" Instead, I made a remark about how they had probably experienced this kind of frustration in communication many times before. They both nodded their heads in agreement.

Defining Defensiveness

Defensive communication is not an isolated problem experienced by only a few couples. Virtually all marriages have moments when this trait prevails. While it is nice to fantasize about ideal marital interaction, each of us can humbly admit to times when we have acted imperfectly with our spouses. No one has a perfect marriage. After all, when two sinful people join in marital union, the sinful nature doesn't disappear. It merely has new ways to exhibit itself. So we should not be unduly alarmed when defensiveness occurs. We need to make allowance for this imperfection even as we seek to overcome it.

Defensiveness is defined as a feeling of resistance caused by conflict and frustration. It is a tactic used, presumably, to relieve the individual from anxiety, since it prompts one to take protective measures to shield oneself from a perceived threat. This behavior is intricately connected to the self-preserving mechanism that has been placed inside each person by God. (Just as we have natural physical protective behaviors, such as blinking and flinching, we also have natural psychological protective behaviors.) It is only fair to note that defensiveness is not always illogical. It is a means of guarding one's psychological self.

The problem with defensiveness, however, is that most of us tend to misuse it, considerably. When we are defensively, we tend not to have the loving, constructive mindset that is vital to marital harmony. Because of this, our use of defensive behavior tends to work in an opposite direction from what is desired. That is, while defensive communication may be intended to relieve anxiety, it usually creates more of it. This is because most of our defensiveness is guided by short-term considerations, with not much forethought given to long-term results.

For the most part, defensiveness tends to occur on a subconscious level. It can cause a person to follow a style of interpersonal relating that utilizes denial and sidestepping tactics. As an example, you may point out to your spouse that he or she is acting in an unbecoming manner, and the response may be "I am not!" Defensiveness tends to lack objectivity.

Look back to the illustration of Dick and Lisa. We could say that they each had legitimate reasons for being guarded in their communication style. After all, each was saying some offensive things to the other. Yet, we can also observe that the defensiveness quickly reached such a level that objectivity and harmony were lost almost immediately. While each felt the need for self-protection, the marriage was losing ground. And, to make matters worse, neither was aware of the fact that each of them was only fueling the other's poor communications.

Three Patterns of Defensiveness

No two couples will display their defensiveness in the

same manner. Our personalities are like snowflakes: no two are exactly alike. Therefore we will all handle our emotions and communications differently. Yet, no matter how different people are, there are three basic, observable styles of marital defensiveness to which most marriages are prone. One I call the prosecutor-prosecutor style, another is the prosecutor-defender style, and the last is the defender-defender style. Each style of communication is equally devastating.

In the prosecutor-prosecutor style of communication, both spouses feel a high level of resistance to each other. Thoughts are expressed in a disagreeable manner, and feelings are shared in a "pushy" style. When a couple enters this pattern of communication, *both* partners defend themselves by taking the offensive. Both indulge in openly exchanging accusing words, threats, and anger. Each makes an all-out effort to change the other person's perspective. The prosecutor-prosecutor style of communication lives by the creed: "The best defense is a good offense." As you might imagine, this pattern often ends in ugly fights.

Case Example
Prosecutor-prosecutor style

Glen and Sharon were both highly verbal individuals. In social surroundings, both could be counted on to make pleasant conversation. Neither was the type of person to hold in opinions and feelings. So naturally, when disagreements arose in their family life, both could be counted on to contribute their "two cents worth." As their neighbors would testify, when they argued, they *argued*. Each would expend enormous amounts of energy trying to get the other to see things from the "right" point of view. Consequently, their disagreements tended to have an extremely distasteful nature and each rarely felt satisfied that the other spouse truly understood. Their arguments resembled a competition to see who could out-convince the other.

The prosecutor-defender style of communication, on the other hand, is enacted when one partner tends to be talkative while the other hides behind a wall of evasiveness. In this pattern, one spouse expends a large amount of emotional energy pleading and cajoling, while the other works equally as hard in trying to sidestep the communication process. One is clearly more insistent, while the other is clearly more resistant. The prosecutor's primary aim is to prove that he or she has legitimate thoughts and feelings, while the defender's primary aim is to wriggle out of the conflict.

When a couple enters the prosecutor-defender style of communication, they usually find themselves interacting on entirely different mental levels. For example, a husband may be trying to express his convictions regarding a financial decision, while his wife responds that she thinks he is talking too loudly and should lower his voice. Not only is the communication focused on different subjects, but they are on entirely different dimensions of thought. One is sharing thoughts and feelings; the other is attuned only to the tone of voice with which the words are spoken. It is easy to understand why this pattern ends, virtually always, in a cold stalemate.

Case Example
Prosecutor-defender style

Debbie and Lance were opposite personality types. Debbie was vivacious and enjoyed those special moments when she was able to share feelings and experiences on an intimate level with close friends. She was strongly committed to her Christian beliefs and desperately desired a home atmosphere in which she could openly discuss those beliefs. Lance, on the other hand, was more closed when personal and philosophical issues arose. He enjoyed a good chat about politics or sports, but he just didn't "get into" feelings and intimacy. Also, he was the type of person whose idea of a pleasant evening at home was to sit quietly in front of the TV. Debbie liked activity.

With such differences, it would be predictable that their communication styles were quite distracting to each other. When problems or personal issues arose, Debbie usually seemed to be the pursuer. She had many matters she wanted to discuss. It was easy for her to assume that Lance should also want to open up. Consequently, she tended to come across as the prosecutor pleading her case. Of course, that didn't sit well with Lance. He would usually try to carry on with his mundane household routines so he could dodge Debbie's questions and statements. He would say things like: "Just quit worrying about things so much," or "Don't expect me to argue with you, because I won't." His communication style was that of the defender hiding behind evasive tactics.

Finally, the defender-defender style of communication is one in which both partners spend great amounts of time keeping their thoughts and feelings strictly to themselves. Neither is prone to open confrontation, so there is little arguing in this pattern. Rather, a couple who exhibits the defender-defender pattern will quickly agree that they have virtually no productive communication in their home. In this pattern there are plenty of empty feelings, but there seems to be an unspoken agreement between the spouses that neither will dare to stir the waters by bringing painful subjects into conversation. As a result, the relationship is marked by extreme superficiality.

Case Example
Defender-defender style

Candice and Bob had been married for over twenty years. If ever asked about the nature of their marriage, they could honestly report that they rarely argued. On the surface, that might sound wonderful. But, in truth, theirs was not a wonderful marriage. You see, it was true that they rarely shared any feelings with each other. Their relationship could best be described as a "roommate marriage."

When they came home from their respective jobs each evening, little would be said beyond "Hi, how was your day?" After dinner, each would go to a separate end of the house. Candice would read or write letters back in the bedroom and Bob would watch TV or occasionally go outside and play tennis. On weekends they shared very few activities. The only time they seemed to spend together was when they went to one of their children's athletic events. Beyond that, their relationship was nil.

In the defender-defender relationship, both spouses hold their feelings close to the belt. Little is shared and little is resolved. On the surface it tends to be a calm relationship. But, beneath the surface, both tend to have deeply buried feelings of frustration.

Virtually no couple enjoys the results of defensive interchanges. Whether the couple utilizes the prosecutor-prosecutor style, prosecutor-defender style, or the defender-defender style, the end result is the same. There are hurt feelings and love is tarnished. It is safe to say that God never intended a man and a woman to interact within patterns of communication that lead to such frustration. In fact, his desire is that we work diligently to pursue a lifestyle founded on biblical principles of harmony.

The Need for Harmony

Each human has been created for the purpose of having relationships. First, God desires that we each develop a personal relationship with him. No other opportunity on earth is more important or more potentially rewarding. Second, he desires that we seek to develop love and harmony with fellow humans, beginning with family relations. By enjoying harmony on the human level, we are then more able to experience the harmony that God desires us to have with him on the spiritual level. This is all part of his divine plan.

In Scripture, we are told what God desires of us:

> Let us continually offer up a sacrifice of praise to God, that is, the fruit of lips that give thanks to His name. And do not neglect doing good and sharing (Heb. 13:15-16).
> Let us not become boastful, challenging one another (Gal. 5:26).
> Bear one another's burdens, and thus fulfill the law of Christ (Gal. 6:2).
> Let all be harmonious, sympathetic, brotherly, kind-hearted, and humble in spirit; not returning evil for evil,

or insult for insult, but giving a blessing instead; for you were called for the very purpose that you might inherit a blessing (1 Peter 3:8-9).

God has placed each human on this earth for a very specific purpose (to have a relationship with him and to have relationships with others), and he has given us a plan. His plan calls for the giving and receiving of such things as kindness, understanding, and concern. And since marriage is the most significant human relationship, it stands to gain the most when his plan is enacted. But it can also lose the most when we pursue counter plans.

Let's go back to the original illustration of Dick and Lisa. I'd like to share with you what happened to them as they continued in their counseling and in their efforts to change their communication habits.

We spent the bulk of the initial session discussing how they had never intended to have an aura of defensiveness in their marriage. We noted how they had begun the marriage with the best of intentions, but through the years they had allowed a pattern of "stonewalling" to creep in. Along the way there had been other problems, such as a misuse of anger, decreased interest in sexual relations, and harsh judgments and criticisms. They didn't know exactly how they had managed to paint themselves in such a corner, but they were both more than ready to take a different route in their relationship.

As I talked with Dick and Lisa, I explained that there was a definite way out of this trap of defensiveness, but it would take much concentration and deliberate effort. They would need to examine such factors as their separate uses of anger, their guiding philosophies of communication, and their overall goals for the relationship. Progress couldn't come to them in one swoop, but they could witness improvements if they would stick with it. By the end of the session they each were relatively calm and ready to chart a new course toward harmony. Neither of them wanted to continue in a marriage that resembled a courtroom scene, complete with a prosecutor and a defense attorney. There in my office they each openly committed themselves to learn how to have harmony in their communications based on the reliable principles found in the Bible.

As time progressed, Lisa spent hours examining why she so readily threw up the walls of defensiveness and why she was often quick to be a prosecutor. Likewise, Dick looked at himself in a way that he had never done to determine how he came to be so edgy and prone to sulking. They both discovered that they had failed to fully understand and control old thinking and behavioral patterns learned in their earlier years. Expectations of an ideal marriage had been nurtured in each of their minds and misconceptions regarding the use of such things as anger had abounded. They learned that it was possible to control their defensive habits if they would do three things:

1. Learn to think through the meaning of their communication habits with regard to their feelings of self-esteem (or lack of it).
2. Recognize the need to drop rigid expectations long enough to be good listeners, thinking through the other person's point of view.
3. Reevaluate their Christian beliefs, with the idea of making those beliefs consistent with their behavior.

Dick and Lisa would be the first to admit that in order to break the pattern of defensive communication, they needed a thorough understanding of why they had certain feelings and behaviors. Then, once they had a better grasp of why they did what they did, they needed specific guidelines that would point them in the direction of harmony.

In the chapters to follow, there will be four sections, each dealing with a specific aspect of marital communication. First, you will be encouraged to examine yourself and your marriage in order to identify the level of defensiveness in your communications. As you are able to have specific identification in this area, your ability to improve will increase. Second is an explanation of why defensiveness occurs. You will have a chance to explore the various factors that contribute to defensive patterns. Third, we will examine different thoughts and concepts that can lead to an atmosphere of marital harmony. In this section we will draw from the teachings of the Bible in order to discover God's plan for marital relationships. Then, finally, we will draw some positive conclusions regarding how to put harmony into your marital communications.

My sincere desire is that you will learn about yourself and God's plan for your marriage so you can experience the pleasure he intends you to have.

Part One

Identifying
Defensiveness

1

Defensiveness Is a Choice

Most couples will admit that it is very uncomfortable to be in a guarded posture toward one's mate. The vast majority of people who find themselves in a marriage that has a defensive atmosphere are frustrated, to say the least. This is only natural, because defensiveness does little to generate a feeling of pleasure in a relationship. Let's put it this way: I have yet to meet the couple who has said, "Boy, I'd really like to have a relationship where we constantly felt like we had to keep our guards up. Wouldn't it be neat to be irritated with each other for long stretches of time!" It would seem safe to say that no sane person would deliberately choose such a style of communication.

But let's examine something carefully. Have you ever thought of defensiveness as being a pattern of choice? On the surface, it would seem odd that anyone would choose to live in a defensive marriage. Yet, most of us would agree that defensiveness doesn't just *happen*. What would you think if I suggested that defensiveness occurs as an act of the will?

It's true. When defensiveness occurs, it is due to specific, willful decisions. Sometimes defensive behavior is so habitual that we are no longer conscious of the decisions we are making. Yet, if we are very thorough in our self-examination, we will recognize that every time defensive behavior occurs, a decision to do so is made first. So, in order to gain mastery over this communication style, we must readily acknowledge that it is something within the realm of our willful controls.

In virtually everything we do we make choices. For example, we choose how friendly we will be, we choose how often we will speak kindly, we choose to listen or to tune out. We choose how we will interact. In order to better illustrate this point, think to yourself about a time recently when you acted in a resistant manner and then see if you can pinpoint the decision you made that led to that behavior. Perhaps you can recall a time when your spouse corrected you regarding an error you made, and you were not in a particularly receptive frame of mind. You may have thought to yourself: "Why should I be the one to change my behavior? I'm tired of being told what I ought to be doing." So in a split second you made the decision: "I'm not going to put up with this. I think I'll tell my spouse to get off my back." This decision process may have been lightning quick, but it was very much in action. Your communication style was enacted by a willful choice.

One of the key characteristics that separates humans from other created beings is that we each have a free will. God has created each person with the ability to think through matters of right and wrong. He wants us to behave according to our own personal choices because, when we do so, life has more depth and more potential meaning. When we lose sight of this crucial fact about free will, our behaviors and communications can resemble the knee reflex. That is, they can become so automatic that our lives can be conducted with little guidance by the conscious mind. To be sure, the choices are still made, but they are made "underground."

Creating Defensiveness

With this in mind, I would like to illustrate how a person can deliberately determine to create an atmosphere of defensiveness. Perhaps by examining some of the steps involved in creating such an atmosphere, it will help you in your efforts toward self-examination. You may then conclude that, if it is possible to choose defensiveness as a dominant lifestyle, it would also be possible to choose to be a harmonizer. (You may not choose that, but that's up to you.)

Following are twelve suggestions regarding how to create a defensive atmosphere in your marriage. If you decide that you really want to erect walls of resistance in your home, you will be successful if you apply these guidelines:

1. Have a long list of expectations for your spouse. As a first step toward creating an atmosphere of defensiveness in your home, you can choose to draw up an agenda of "do's" and "don'ts" for your spouse. The longer the list, the better. As you communicate your feelings and needs with your spouse, keep preconceived notions in your mind regarding how your spouse is supposed to respond. Expect your spouse to neatly fit the mold you have designed for him or her. As this happens, you will become guided by idealistic dreams and will quickly lose touch with the reality that no human is perfect. Then, to add icing to the cake, when your spouse falls short of these expectations, quickly point it out. Keep your spouse on edge, like he or she is walking on eggshells. Make it your goal to communicate perfectionistic notions, and then you will be well on your way in your efforts to create walls of resistance.

2. *Assume that all anger is bad and that you should never disagree.* The next step toward creating a defensive atmosphere is to be highly threatened by anger. Certainly you have witnessed how anger can be abused and expressed in destructive ways. Perhaps you have been on the receiving end of someone else's distasteful anger, or maybe you have been guilty of inappropriate uses of it yourself. So, before looking at any constructive purposes that can be found in assertive, biblical anger, simply write off the whole emotion. Dismiss all anger as a nasty emotion. Make no acknowledgement for the fact that couples need to air out their feelings (constructively) with each other. Look only at the fact that anger is an uncomfortable emotion and try to avoid it with no further thought.

3. *Use the word* you *frequently, particularly during disagreements.* Want to keep your partner back-pedaling? All you have to do is use one tiny word over and over. It's the word *you*. For example: "What's wrong with you anyway?" or "If only you would . . ." or "You never . . . ." Make your partner assume that all you ever think about is his or her flaws. By keeping the focus of communication on your spouse, you can become highly successful in creating a very offensive style of interaction, which of course leads directly to defensive comebacks. Whatever you do, don't put the focus on yourself whenever marital tensions arise, at least, not if you're aiming for a defensive atmosphere. Don't say things like "I think we need to examine how I can contribute to a more pleasant atmosphere." Keep the focus outward, not inward.

4. *Keep secrets.* As a further means of creating a defensive atmosphere, have a hidden aspect to your personality that you wouldn't dare share with anyone else, even your spouse. Work hard to create that certain image that you

feel will bring the most compliments and will keep you out of trouble. Reveal only flattering facts about yourself and keep all negative experiences inside. This will keep you busy fending off the possibility that others may break down the image you have created. Even if this creates a feeling of phoniness, keep it up. After all, in creating a lifestyle of defensiveness, phoniness is a good aid.

In addition to keeping secrets about yourself, you can also make it necessary for your spouse to do the same. Don't accept unflattering facts about your spouse. If he or she ever exposes a personal weakness or a negative feeling, express shock and try to induce a feeling of shame. Hold firmly to the notion that openness regarding the negative side of life has no place in your marriage.

5. Worry about what others might think of you. As a corollary to keeping secrets, you can create a defensive atmosphere by choosing to be highly sensitive, to the point of strong worry, with regard to the opinions and reactions of others. Develop such a concern for the thoughts of others that you allow your actions to be dictated by "public opinion." Mull over and over in your mind what terrible things someone else could think about you. To do this, you will need to think negative, even derogatory thoughts about yourself. Get it fixed in your mind that you are a fragile person who would fall to pieces if anyone really knew the real you. Assume that you occupy an inferior position in life and that a more "polished" person is superior to you. By becoming a worried, nervous person, you will be assured of creating an uptight, tense environment.

6. Develop legalistic religious beliefs. If you are choosing to be one who creates a defensive atmosphere, then seek to be "religious," rather than pursuing a lifestyle that exhibits the fruit of the Spirit (see Gal. 5:22-23). Be one who makes pious duties and obligations out of every aspect of family life. Make it a chore to be patient. Insist that everyone in your household should be loving. Be hard-headed . . . but do it in the name of the Lord.

There is a very distinct difference between a Spirit-filled Christian and a religious legalist. Whereas a spiritual person will seek to pursue traits such as patience and gentleness out of a genuine desire, a religious person is one who does those things because that's what the rulebook says you're supposed to do. This legalist usually develops a reputation for being head-strong and unbending. By fervently observing religious "musts," the religious person can behave so piously that the people nearest him or her feel uncomfortable about themselves. Of course, this sense of discomfort is a direct contributor to the defensive pattern.

7. *Sidestep the feedback given to you by others*. Another means of choosing defensiveness is to shun the constructive suggestions given to you by your spouse. Assume that you've gotten your life pretty well in order and you have no real need for any helpful hints. Even though the feedback given you may be positive and lovingly offered, don't accept it. Who knows, if you admit to criticism once, you may just be setting yourself up for more of the same at a later date. Besides, a defensive person, by definition, is one who feels the need to protect him/herself from outside intrusions. And by opening oneself to messages from another person, one would be violating the code of defensive behavior. Therefore, if you genuinely choose to be a resister, you can use phrases such as: "Don't bug me, I'm busy now," or "How many times do I have to tell you that I'm just not in the mood to talk things over now?"

8. *Hold firmly to traditions*. A defensive person is one who likes to keep things controlled and predictable. Flexibility regarding new and different things is not a com-

mon trait among chronic resisters. Consequently, defensive people often choose to cling tightly to the past. They regularly handle today's problems by thinking about how things used to be. Little effort is made to accommodate one's spouse who may simply approach life from a different point of view. The resistant person very often idealizes past traditions to the extent that anything new is perceived as a threat. If someone asks this person why he or she persists in holding on to old ways, the answer usually comes back, "That's just the way I've always done things."

9. *Be lazy.* Laziness is a form of self-absorption. When a person goes into a lazy mode of behavior, there is little openness to the needs of others. And since that's what defensiveness is all about, you can see how laziness can be a successful means of keeping people at arm's length. When choosing this form of resistance, there are many ways to act upon your laziness. For example, you can choose to be a procrastinator, putting off chores and responsibilities. You can tune your family out as you become wrapped up in reading the newspaper. You could decide to become addicted to TV or you might allow yourself to get involved with trashy novels and magazines. There is an endless number of opportunities to help you achieve laziness.

10. *Seek to be in control of minor things.* As a further means of establishing a defensive atmosphere, you might decide to become a nit-picker. Be bossy, particularly in minor matters. Be finicky in the way you like to have things kept at your house. Hover over your spouse until you get the compliance from him or her that you feel you need. As you develop a reputation as a critic and a pessimist, you will find that open communications are next to impossible. Naturally, this would be a defensive person's delight. The person who insists on having small matters

go exactly as he or she prescribes is guaranteed to create an aura of distastefulness. I might add, not only can you seek to be in control of external details, but you can also do this with your spouse's inner traits. That is, you can pick at your spouse's personality quirks and minor flaws.

11. Have conditional acceptance. In order to have a successful and harmonious marriage, acceptance is a necessary prerequisite. In fact, we could assume that the need to be loved and cherished just as we are is one of the most basic of all human needs. So it would only be logical that, if your goal is to create marital defensiveness, you could choose to offer acceptance only when your conditions are met. In this sense, you would be setting yourself up into a god-like position over your mate. You could be the one to determine whether or not your mate deserves love.

As an example of giving conditional acceptance, you could choose to be kind to your mate only after kindness has been first extended to you. You might choose to give respect and honor to your mate only as your mate gives it to you. Or, when your mate fails you, offer forgiveness only after a sufficient apology is rendered. Feel proud that you make others earn your love.

12. Focus so heavily on issues of right and wrong that you lose your sense of compassion. Some issues are black and white. There are times when you know you are right and your spouse is wrong, and there is no convincing you of anything otherwise. For example, you may be a wife who is offended by your husband's occasional crude remarks. Or perhaps you are a husband who has to tolerate times when your wife ignores you. You know your spouse is wrong. There's no question about it! So what do you do at a time like this?

If you are making a deliberate attempt to create an atmosphere of defensiveness, you can latch on to your correct convictions and run them straight into the ground. That is, when you are right and your spouse is wrong, you can develop a very insistent style of communication. You might clam up in stern silence until your partner finally sees things your way. You may decide to back your spouse into a corner with a barrage of loaded questions. Or you may choose to lecture on and on to your spouse about the wrongness of his or her ways. Repeat to yourself over and over how inappropriate your spouse's actions are. Never mind that you are being disgustingly angry as you insist on what is right. If defensiveness is your goal, you won't worry about speaking diplomatically.

When the twelve steps mentioned here are followed closely, a defensive marital atmosphere is guaranteed. The walls of resistance will be so thick that harmony would never be achieved. It is important to note that each of the twelve steps can be a choice. You can decide to proceed in this manner, or you can decide to refrain. (I must admit, some people are so skilled in creating defensiveness that they do so with little conscious thought.) The style in which you relate to your spouse is a matter of the will. The decision to be or not to be an appropriate communicator is entirely up to you.

Let me share an illustration of a couple who chose to hone their defensive "skills" to near-perfection.

Case Example

When Mark and Jan met each other thirteen years ago their relationship really took off. Jan saw in Mark a handsome young man who seemed to have a sensitivity that other men she had dated lacked. He was winsome with his easy smile, and he quickly put her at ease. In turn, Mark's perception was that Jan was a sweet, supportive woman who was willing to set her needs aside in favor of showing kindness to him. She would do special little favors, like making him cookies regularly. That really impressed him! During the first year of their relationship, they shared many pleasant moments. Except for a few minor squabbles they got along splendidly. As they looked toward the future, both had said it was quite bright.

But that was thirteen years ago. Now, after eleven years of marriage, they tell an entirely different story. No longer are Mark's and Jan's days marked by the pleasantness of that early period. Rather, they spend a large portion of their time avoiding each other. Or at least, they avoid speaking about personal feelings or subjects that would be potentially controversial. You see, when Mark and Jan began their relationship, they may have had high regard for each other, but they also had very high expectations—unbearably high expectations. They each had many unspoken thoughts about what the other should be. At first, they were on such good behavior that their expectations seemed reasonable. But with the hum-drum days of living in a family routine, they each slowly began to realize that the other wasn't going to "fit the mold." Neither felt that the other was responding in feelings and communication the way they were "supposed to." To Jan, Mark didn't turn out to be quite the sensitive person she had assumed he was. As far as she was concerned, he spent too many hours in meaningless activity (like TV), and he habitually tuned her out. And from Mark's perspective, Jan wasn't as interested in him as he thought she should be. It seemed that she was just interested in making him do exactly what she wanted him to do. You might say they were playing a psychological game of tug-of-war.

Mark's and Jan's problem was that when the differences in their personalities had become more and more obvious, rather than looking for ways to pursue harmony, both husband and wife chose to dig in their heels in a stand of resistance. Whenever disagreements arose, both would stubbornly maneuver to try to prove how the other should feel or behave differently. Each would focus on the other's need to change, not on his or her own need. Mark was a forceful debator, so he would use his skills in logic to try to coerce Jan into his way of thinking. Jan realized that she could gain power over her husband by being evasive whenever Mark made his attempts to change her. She might use tactics like leaving the room or saying "I don't want to talk about it."

The most puzzling aspect of Mark's and Jan's problem was that they were each consciously aware that they were creating a defensive atmosphere in their home. Both would admit that they didn't like the turmoil this brought. Yet neither was truly willing to be the one to break down the walls of defensiveness. They were each too invested in their "right" ways to soften. Consequently, a stalemate occurred and both were left with buried feelings of anger regarding the marriage.

In marital communications, nothing happens merely by chance. We each have reasons for interacting in our various styles. The problem is that, when we act negatively, we may be making decisions that we are not even consciously aware of. When this happens, our emotions (not our minds) are in charge of our communications. That is, our words and deeds may erupt so quickly that we don't adequately think through the reasoning behind our actions.

We tend to be creatures of habit. And once we become accustomed to making certain decisions regarding communication, our minds can go into "automatic pilot." That is why it is so vitally important to examine the potential choices (such as the ones mentioned in this chapter) that we have. Awareness of what we are deciding upon is the crucial first step in making positive changes. As the awareness of our decisions increases, our ability to reasonably think through the goals of our communications also increases.

2

Examine Yourself!

In the last chapter, I mentioned that it is crucial to note that we are all capable of choosing our communication styles. Having an awareness of our choices is a crucial first step in overcoming problems. People who are willing to submit to an honest appraisal of themselves are the ones who are likely to grow. It is frustrating enough for a person to live with a closed, resistant style of communication. But it can become even worse if that person chooses to do little or no self-examination.

Second Corinthians 13:5 states: "Test yourselves to see if you are in the faith; examine yourselves!" Just as a store owner periodically takes inventory of the goods on his shelves, it is helpful for each of us to take an inventory of our personality traits. The worst thing that can happen to a couple who wishes to have a prosperous marriage is they grow smug and complacent about themselves. A periodic, healthy looking-over of one's tendencies is good lubrication for a marriage. It keeps the cogs of progress turning.

In order to gain a good idea of your level of defensiveness, it would be helpful for you to complete the following inventory. By determining the amount of defensiveness you exhibit, you can become motivated positively toward making the appropriate changes.

Defensiveness Quiz

Complete each question as quickly as you can. Your first reaction is usually the best.

1. Even though I am hesitant to openly admit it, I have a definite list of expectations regarding the way I think my spouse should treat me.   T   F

2. When things don't go my way, I'm not above putting on an old-fashioned pout.   T   F

3. I feel uneasy when I am not in control of things.   T   F

4. The people who know me best would say that they have to be very careful about the way they offer suggestions to me.   T   F

5. I have had fairly significant bouts with feelings of inferiority.   T   F

6. There have been times when I have dreamed of packing my bags and running away from home.   T   F

7. There are times when I feel that my spouse owes me more than he or she has actually given me.   T   F

8. When my spouse and I disagree, I can become pretty stubborn.   T   F

9. I have been accused of coming across like a "know-it-all."   T   F

10. When my spouse makes errors I find it very difficult to refrain from saying something about it. T F

11. When my spouse gives me criticisms, I feel it necessary to offer an excuse. T F

12. I don't like to be in new surroundings. T F

13. When someone else is acting in an unbecoming way, I usually find myself looking for a way to avoid that person. T F

14. It is not unusual for me to become moody, even with little provocation. T F

15. Once I open myself up to someone, I demand loyalty from that person. T F

16. My spouse thinks that I am too argumentative. T F

17. I am probably too sensitive for my own good. T F

18. Once I become engrossed in a project (a hobby, chore, watching TV, etc.) it is common for me to just tune other people out. T F

19. I really don't like the thought of having to work toward a good marriage. T F

20. When problems occur in our marriage, I usually look first to see what my spouse has done wrong. T F

21. I am prone to using sarcastic words and overtones in my speech. T F

22. I really hate to admit when I'm wrong. T F

23. It is not uncommon for me to feel frustrated, even when I look calm on the outside. T F

24. In my past I had an overabundance of strict discipline and control. T F

25. I'm afraid to let my spouse know the real me.   T   F

26. I have had secret sexual thoughts that no one else knows about.   T   F

27. For as long as I can remember, anger has been an emotion that has brought nothing but unpleasantness my way.   T   F

28. It really bothers me to know that someone else is wrong.   T   F

29. Impatience is a trait that I know well.   T   F

30. I spend little or no time thinking deeply about God's purpose for my life.   T   F

31. The word *should* is an often-used word in my vocabulary.   T   F

32. I have a hard time sharing intimate feelings with others.   T   F

33. Currently, I have fewer than five close friends or associates.   T   F

34. It is not uncommon for me to use humor to sidestep delicate matters.   T   F

35. Most of the time I'm preoccupied with striving for success.   T   F

36. My spouse would say that I become grumpy and edgy too easy.   T   F

37. I have had struggles recently with feelings of loneliness.   T   F

38. The moods of other people tend to affect me greatly.   T   F

39. I have perfectionistic notions about the ideal marriage.   T   F

40. When I see other happy couples, my heart aches with a yearning to have a better marriage.   T   F

41. My sense of pride can become hurt fairly easily. T F

42. It is not unusual for me to procrastinate when I have minor chores to do. T F

43. I'm not above using the silent treatment when a discussion is not going my way. T F

44. I have a bad habit of letting my feelings fester inside, not letting go very easily. T F

45. There are times when I can become down-right lazy. T F

46. I really enjoy watching TV and, in fact, could spend several hours at a time in front of the television set. T F

47. I have a problem with thinking too many critical thoughts. T F

48. I'm not very likely to share personal thoughts and feelings with others in a very intimate way. T F

49. I have been known to tell lies in order to cover up character flaws. T F

50. When it comes to demonstrating kindness and love, I tend not to be the initiator. Rather, I usually wait for my spouse to set the pace in his area. T F

51. When I am in a group of people, I am usually hesitant to share my thoughts or to ask questions. T F

52. I have periodic bouts with feelings of depression. T F

53. I do not have a strong feeling of being supported by my spouse or by close friends. T F

54. I have a hard time relating well to children. T F

55. My real preference is to be left alone rather than being around people. T F

56. I can intellectualize with almost anyone, but I don't share feelings well. T F

57. I worry too much about my public image. T F

58. I often look for secret ways to dodge responsibilities (in chores, in sharing personal struggles etc.). T F

59. I automatically become resistant when my spouse feels angry. T F

60. When I speak about personal matters, I do so slowly and hesitantly. T F

Now, go back and count the number of times you marked T as your response. This will tell you how seriously you need to confront the issue of defensiveness.

If you scored less than fifteen, you are probably a very open, gregarious person. You probably are socially adept and you're the kind of person who can easily calm excited nerves. (Either that or you used quite a bit of denial.) Go back over your responses and see if you can pinpoint aspects of your communication style that can become even better.

If you scored between fifteen and thirty, you are probably in the normal range of defensiveness. We all will be prone to defensiveness from time to time, so this should cause no serious alarm. However, you will have the task of becoming more flexible in the way you respond to your mate. Since you have a fair amount of defensiveness already, it would be easy for your weak spots to get out of hand during tense circumstances.

Those of you who scored between thirty-one and forty-five have probably experienced some fairly significant communication problems already. There is a good chance that you have had more than your share of marital frustration. Your closest relationships may not be as open and rewarding as you would like. You will need extra amounts of concentration as you learn to set aside old habits, becoming a harmonizer instead.

If you scored forty-six or more, you should probably seek marital counseling quickly. If you are in this range, there is probably a tight atmosphere at home. You may or may not have frequent arguments, but it is highly likely that little closeness is shared. Your task is great, but it is certainly not impossible.

If you would like to check the accuracy of your score, you might ask your spouse to take this test as if it were you responding. That is, your spouse can answer the questions from your point of view. You'll probably learn some interesting things about how you are perceived by your spouse. It should be revealing! Once your spouse completes the test, take an average of your two scores and you should have very accurate results.

Keep in mind the purpose of this inventory. It is meant to increase your level of self-awareness. As you pinpoint the areas in your communication style that can be improved, your level of marital satisfaction can also increase.

3

The Wide World
of Defensiveness

Defensiveness is an extremely broad-based characteristic. It can be manifested in so many different ways that it boggles the mind! Some forms of defensiveness are so obvious that virtually anyone would be able to spot them. Yet other manifestations of this trait are so subtle that we may be unaware of the way in which we create resistance in communication. In such cases we experience frustration in our relationship without fully understanding why.

In this chapter we will continue the effort to identify defensive communications by examining the many ways they can be enacted. Their manifestations fall into three separate categories: (1) denial, (2) "boomerang" communication, and (3) evasiveness. As you continue to open your mind to this trait, you will become more able to make constructive adjustments when the need arises.

Denial Defensiveness

There are times when marital partners feel so uncomfortable about their own flawed behaviors and feelings that they choose to ignore their presence. At those times, denial is the defensive maneuver most likely to be used. Denial is defined as the refusal to acknowledge or recognize a personal problem or a legitimate allegation offered by another person. Behaviors in this category are often enacted by subconscious motivations.

Case Example

Denny was a man who found it extremely difficult to admit a personal flaw. Whenever a problem situation arose at home, he was usually very clever in separating himself from any responsibility for that problem. It's not that he was deliberately attempting to be "slippery." Rather, he honestly didn't think he made errors in his personal relationships. So he reasoned that, if trouble arose, he must not have had anything to do with it. Naturally, his wife stayed chronically frustrated with this man who would admit to no wrong.

As it turns out, Denny was reared in a home where mistakes absolutely were not tolerated. Because of this, he had learned how to "toe the line," keeping his behavior clean and beyond questioning. Then, as he entered his career, Denny found that he was frequently under public scrutiny. Now he had more reason to hide his faults and expose only the positive side of his personality. What Denny failed to realize was that he had made defensive behavior such a habit that it had silently worked its way into his entire personality and lifestyle.

The regular use of denial in one's personal relationships will usually lead to the problem of stagnation in one's personal development. Little or no growth will occur in the individual's maturity and a superficiality in considering and reacting to serious matters is likely to result. This is because the person using denial simply refuses to comprehend the need for personal development.

Following are some common behaviors used by people who tend to use denial as a means of resisting discomfort in interpersonal relations:

Rationalization

Do you know what it's like to talk with someone who seems to have an airtight explanation for virtually everything? It's frustrating, to say the least! If ever situations arise that might cause such persons to be seen in an unfavorable light, they automatically use rationalization to exonerate themselves. Using a long list of reasons, they can tell you why they are innocent of any negative implications. Rationalizers are people who are able to invent a seemingly logical and acceptable explanation for behavior that is unacceptable. In so doing, rationalizers intellectualize feelings to the extent that they are eventually suppressed and avoided. Consequently, such persons are likely to repeat the same old mistakes over and over. There is rarely a time when a weakness is truly admitted. As an example, persons who are perennially critical might say: "I'm not really a critic. It's just that a lot of the things my spouse does are wrong and I can't help but notice them." As you can see, such persons completely sidestep responsibility for their own actions.

Projection

There are times when a person has a character flaw that he or she would rather not admit, so instead of openly dealing with the flaw, he or she may focus on it as it exists in someone else. When this occurs, the denial defense of *projection* is being used.

Keep in mind that when a person uses one of the defenses of denial regularly, that person's goal is total avoidance of any identification with personal weakness. So what better way is there to avoid examination of oneself than to put the spotlight elsewhere? When this is done, one's mental energies are completely spent on someone else's problems, and the projector is able to feel smug due to the fact that a feeling of "one-up" can come by putting others "in their place."

As an example of projection, picture an insecure wife who says, "I just can't believe that my husband doesn't notice my needs. He really has problems of insecurity." She shifts the focus to her husband with no conscious recognition of the glaring inconsistency in such a statement.

Magical Thinking

No one enjoys having problems. In fact, when a difficulty occurs, the most natural thing to do is to look for the solution. So when a problem occurs where there is no positive solution in sight, some people are prone to kidding themselves into thinking that everything will work out just fine. Rather than facing reality head on, some individuals feel the necessity to fabricate stories in which everything works to a perfect ending. They use *magical thinking*.

For example, I remember counseling with a woman whose husband had been sexually unfaithful many times over the span of several years. This woman was a very insecure person who could not bear the thought of confronting her husband about this. She adopted the attitude that he would eventually straighten out this problem if she continued to pray for him, so she never confronted him with her feelings.

In doing this, she denied that his infidelity posed a problem to her. Rather, she claimed that as long as he had his difficulties, she would just learn to be a more patient person. This woman's story of prayer and patience sounded nice, yet it was clear that she was clinging to an illusion in order to avoid the hurt and loneliness that would accompany an honest appraisal of her marriage.

The "Ain't Life Grand" Syndrome

A man once came to my counseling office stating that he had been living in an unhappy marriage for years. He said he was suffering from depression and was finding less and less motivation to live. I asked if he would bring his wife to the office on his next visit so that I could get some input from her.

The next week, when I met the wife, I was greeted by a bubbly, happy-go-lucky woman who seemed to have no cares or burdens in the world. When I asked her to share her feelings about their marriage, she told me that she was as happy as a woman could be. She said she and her husband got along splendidly with one another.

As she spoke, I began to get a better understanding of her husband's frustration. This wife was so resistant to facing any negative aspects of marriage that she had made a decision to completely *ignore the negative* and emphasize positive feelings only. In so doing, an atmosphere of rigidity and unreality had resulted. The husband's depression was directly attributable to the fact that, in their home, problems were never addressed and consequently never solved.

A person who chooses to project an image of a life that has never had a hitch is a person who feels (either consciously or subconsciously) totally inadequate in dealing with the discomforts of an imperfect life. So, rather than humbly admitting such feelings, this person plays a game of pretending that life is nothing but a bed of roses. Even when the person is under severe strain, he or she always exhibits predictable enthusiasm and exuberance when asked how things are going. The simple truth is that the *Ain't Life Grand* syndrome is really only a protective guard used by a person who is afraid of feeling hurt.

Playing Incompetent

The Bible says that each person who trusts in Christ has all the strength needed to face trying situations. (See Philippians 4:13.) Be that as it may, there are some people who stubbornly choose to avoid responsibilities by hiding behind a veil of incompetence. The use of the word *can't* is common to them. These people tend to place themselves in a childlike position by playing incompetent. They assume that, if there is a problem to be solved, then someone else is going to have to come along to make things right. When this occurs, the so-called incompetent person is presumably absolved of responsibilities and the burden of resolution is successfully shifted elsewhere.

As an example, picture an exasperated husband who says, "You can't expect me to be kind when my wife is constantly upset about something!" In making such a statement, this husband insinuates that any unkindness on his part is not his problem or responsibility. By assuming an inability to be kind, in light of his wife's behavior, he is avoiding the real issue—his behavior and attitudes.

Countering

Another defensive behavior of denial is *countering*. When a person uses this tactic, there is a refusal to acknowledge a truth or perception given by one's spouse. For example, a husband may say to his wife, "You're acting pretty impatient right now. Let's try to be more tolerant of one another." The wife may quickly respond: "I'm not being impatient. I can't imagine why you say things like that!"

When countering occurs, the defensive person automatically assumes that the perception of the other person is invalid. There is no effort to think about the feedback given to objectively determine if there is any truth to it. Rather, there is an instinctive response of self-preservation, regardless of the facts. When countering is used frequently, the individual has the misfortune of repeating the same problems. Because this is a tactic of denial, the defensive person is likely to turn frustrations on the partner rather than questioning him/herself regarding potential changes that might be made.

The "Know-It-All" Attitude

Some people assume a position in life of being so enlightened that no one can tell them anything they don't already know. These people have instant answers to every question, particularly if the question touches on a personal dimension. It is very predictable, then, that these individuals tend to feel above the problems of "common folk." By assuming a position of omniscience (all-knowingness) people with a know-it-all attitude avoid dealing with the nitty-gritty of human struggle.

Picture a husband who will never allow his wife to offer him constructive criticism. With a sense of arrogance he might say to her: "Why should I listen to you tell me what to do; I know what I'm doing and I don't need anyone to correct me." By taking a position of superiority, he successfully removes himself from the burden of being accountable.

Boomerang Defensiveness

A second major category of defensive maneuvers is the category I call *boomerang defensiveness*. In order to get an idea of what this category entails, try to picture the distinctive characteristic of a boomerang. As this unusual object is clasped firmly and tossed into open air, it will whirl rapidly away from the thrower, but it will soon reverse itself and come back to the individual who tossed it. I can recall some funny moments as a boy, dodging and trying to run away from a boomerang that had reversed its motion to "attack" me. As I look back at those scenes, I can appreciate the real danger the boomerang posed. The boomerang's reverse action could actually harm a fellow if he was being too careless.

In marital communication a boomerang-type reaction can occur when one spouse speaks to another. Words may be spoken by one mate to the other only to be thrown back at the person who said them. For example, a wife may suggest to her husband that he should try to be on time for an important date. The husband may quickly toss the suggestion back at her, saying, "You have no right to tell me what time to get home when you're never on time yourself!" In a split second, the words spoken by the wife have been thrown back at her by a husband who is defensively resistant. In a sense, the wife's words have boomeranged on her due to the defensiveness of the husband.

Boomerang defensiveness is defined as a feeling of resistance characterized by throwing the attention back onto one's mate, when that mate is attempting to offer constructive, innocent suggestions. Whereas the defensiveness of denial is likely to result in stagnation and superficiality, the most likely result of boomerang defensiveness is open aggression. With the use of this style of defensiveness, biting words are often spoken and accusations are thrown. Little effort is made to understand another's point of view.

These are some common tactics used in the practice of boomerang defensiveness:

The "What About You" Game

Defensive people have a hard time accepting the fact that they can exhibit characteristics that others find offensive. Often these people have idealistic notions regarding the way they should be perceived. So when another person, particularly a spouse, points out a deficiency or merely makes a suggestion, these individuals' bubbles are burst. Becoming highly offended, they often attempt to dodge the spotlight by quickly putting the focus onto the person who has made the suggestion.

A slick way to do this is to play the "What about you?" game. In asking such a question, the defensive person might succeed in avoiding the real issue of his or her own character and the one offering the feedback is suddenly forced to put the attention on himself.

For example, a husband may ask his wife to be more friendly when they meet with his business associates. In resistance, she may put the focus right back on him by stating: "Me? Be more friendly? How about when you are with my mother? You wouldn't say a nice word to her if I paid you!" As you can tell, the husband's words are shoved back at him before he has time to blink.

Blaming

Another way of defensively taking the focus off self and putting it back onto the spouse is to use blame. By *blaming* one's spouse for one's actions, the individual is seemingly excused of any wrongdoing. People who readily resort to blame are not nearly as interested in pursuing harmony as they are in sidestepping the "bad-guy" label. Usually this person is sensitive to the point of being easily hurt. Blame is a tactic used by a person who has hidden insecurities that stem from underlying feelings of frailty.

Think of a husband who has been home from work for an hour or more. He was in a bad mood at the office and he has carried his bad mood home with him. This causes him to be grumpy with the kids and edgy toward his wife. In a very casual way, his wife says: "You're not in a very good mood, are you?" Not wishing to deal with his wife's simple perception, he growls, "Well, maybe I could be in a better mood if my family would give me a little peace and quiet when I get home." He has taken his wife's words and slung them back at her. As he walks away, the wife feels hurt and is sorry she even tried to communicate with him.

Bringing Up the Past

A close cousin to the tactic of blaming is that of *bringing up the past*. When this occurs, the defensive partner reverses the focus of communication spoken to him or her by reminding the spouse of wrongs previously committed. True to the defensive goal of avoiding self-examination, this tactic successfully serves the defensive person in that it takes the "punch" out of the partner's confrontation and allows the defender the opportunity to take him/herself off the "hot seat." Most people have done things in the past that shed an unflattering light upon themselves, so defensive people don't hesitate to "go for the jugular" by bringing up past flaws, in order to serve their own momentary needs.

As an example, a wife may comment to her husband about the stern tone of voice he used when disciplining the kids. Defensively, the husband may respond: "Don't I recall some times when you raised your voice inappropriately at the children? What about last summer when you went on your screaming tirade?" By bringing up the past, he throws the burden back to his wife and avoids accountability for his current behavior.

Being a Dictator

Some people live by the philosophy that the best defense is a good offense. Their reasoning is that if they can successfully keep other people on their guard, those people won't have the desire or energy to take the offense. This tactic can be illustrated by the hard-nosed husband who is so demanding with his wife that she is afraid to ever openly question him. I once asked the wife of a very strong-willed domineering husband if she would ever stand up to his tyrannical ways. She responded: "Are you kidding? I value my health too much to risk speaking up to my husband!" This woman's husband was so thorough in his style of *being a dictator* that he was able to defend himself from any "attack" before it ever occurred.

It is important to note that gruff, headstrong husbands are not the only ones who use the defensive tactic of being a dictator. You are aware of some wives who have such a critical nature that they rule the roost in their households. Or perhaps you know of a spouse who uses the more subtle approach of being a grumbler and a mutterer. This illustrates that dictators come in all sorts of personality styles.

48

The "If Only" Game

Keep in mind that the goal of boomerang defensiveness is to keep the focus off oneself by shifting the attention toward the other person. Another means to accomplish this is to play the *if only* game. When this game is in use, the defensive individual avoids a mate's suggestion or confrontation by explaining that one's actions are dependent on what that mate does.

For example, a wife may be told by her husband that she is being quite stand-offish to him, to which she replies: "Well, if only I had a more understanding husband I might not be this way." She doesn't deny the reality of her behavior. Rather she places the responsibility for her behavior squarely on the shoulders of her husband.

Evasive Defensiveness

The third major category of defensive behavior is defense by evasion. In the first category discussed, denial, the defensive person was described as one who would not ever consider his own flaws or the feedback given by others. Then, in the category of boomerang defensiveness, we noted how an individual might avoid self-examination by keeping the focus of attention on the other party. Now in this third category, evasive defensiveness, we will see how people can defend themselves by choosing to ignore the problems that they, inwardly, realize are hindrances.

Evasive defensiveness is defined as a conscious, deliberate decision to escape the responsibilities of interpersonal struggles by blatantly and inappropriately avoiding arguments, accusations, or questions. The most common consequence of evasive defensiveness is that it leads to hidden grudges. The person using evasive tactics has conscious grievances against another person, but he or she is choosing to allow feelings to fester secretly. Presumably, this person would prefer the discomfort of inner resentments to the effort of open, honest sharing.

Case Example

Julia's husband rolled his eyes toward the sky as he spoke: "Honey, I just don't know what I can do to get you to talk things over with me. Why won't you just break down a little and share with me what's on your mind?" Julia looked at her husband as if to say that she had already explained herself a hundred times before, meaning she was tired of telling him: "Look, you're the kind of person who likes to talk about things and I'm not. Deep, deep conversations just aren't my thing, so why don't you just leave me alone."

The reason for Julia's evasiveness seemed logical enough to her. She had grown up in a very controlled, safe environment where no one thought to question the standard way of living. Her household had succinct, precise rules and great effort was made by all to live "correctly." As a result, there was rarely any conflict in her childhood years. (There wasn't much depth to Julia's reasoning either, but that was a price she willingly paid.) So it was only natural, when she became an adult and got married, that she expected a continuation of the same pattern. That is, she assumed that she and her husband would readily agree on how life would be lived and little discussion about hurt feelings or contradictory points of view would arise.

As you can imagine, Julia was in for a rude awakening. To her dismay, she learned that she and her husband did not always see eye to eye as she assumed they should. The disagreements they had were usually minor, but she was so intent on having perfect unity that she would become emotionally unravelled when she and her husband were on differing wave lengths. And, to make matters worse, when the need to confront issues arose, Julia opted to be evasive. Rather than struggling with her husband regarding feelings and beliefs, she would deliberately choose to sidestep such matters, because she felt it was unfair to have to work at marriage. Repeatedly, she would shun her husband's efforts to have open discussions about matters that were important to their relationship. Consequently, as time moved on, the tension in their relationship grew.

Evasive maneuvers are quite common in marital communications. By becoming aware of specific ways in which partners shun each other (creating those hidden grudges), choices can be made with regard to the continuation of those tactics. These are some ways in which spouses act evasively defensive:

Clamming Up

The classic way of avoiding the nitty-gritty of marital communications is by using the silent treatment, clamming up. Some defensive people live by the motto: "Rather than making yourself vulnerable, clam up." When a married person uses this technique, he or she usually feels backed up against a wall. Perhaps the spouse has introduced a delicate issue to be discussed, or maybe uncomfortable feelings are being shared. Whatever the case, the defensive partner responds to his or her own feelings of resistance by becoming zipper-lipped. This partner knows that, when feelings and beliefs are exchanged, there will always be the possibility of having to "give in" on one's position. So, they reason, it is safer to say nothing than to risk having to be flexible and conciliatory. In doing so these people illustrate that they are not nearly as interested in marital harmony as they are in winning marital battles.

For example, think of the wife whose husband has been acting impatiently for the entire day. But finally, at the end of the day, he comes to his senses and tries to mend things with his wife. However, she is in no mood to discuss the nature of their relationship, so when he approaches her she thinks to herself: "I'm not going to say a word. I'll just let him squirm." Because she is resistant to her husband's appeals, the uneasy status of their relationship continues and no resolutions are found.

Changing the Subject

Another evasive maneuver frequently used is that of changing the subject. When the topics of discussion get too personal and close to home, the defensive person may opt to steer the conversation in an entirely different direction. The person who uses this technique can be like the man who felt uncomfortable with his own morality. So whenever issues of religious convictions arose in conversations, he would feel the need to interject comments about his tennis game or some other unrelated subject. While he looked to be a friendly, easy-going person on the outside, inwardly he would be struggling with uncomfortable feelings of resistance. Rather than candidly sharing those feelings, he would choose the option of being deceptively manipulative.

In a similar vein, some people are prone to controlling conversation *before* certain uncomfortable issues arise. While their actions may not be as obvious as the person who deliberately changes the subject, the inner struggle is still the same. Feelings of fear or guilt prompt the use of diversionary tactics.

The "I Don't Care" Mentality

Some spouses may claim to have an uncaring attitude toward their mates when in fact the real issue is one of defensiveness. In communications there are often hidden meanings that lie beneath the spoken words. And, in the case of the "I don't care" attitude, the hidden issue often proves to be resistance. In other words, the person who evades communication with this attitude would probably be more honest if he or she would state: "I'm hesitant to become involved because I'm not sure I'm willing to put out the effort it might require." Here, the defensiveness is more obvious.

I once met a man who stated: "I really don't care what my wife thinks about me as long as she just treats me civilly." When I explored with him how he arrived at such a thought I found a different story. He shared with me that he had tried for years to get his wife to fit the mold of what he thought she should be. But inevitably such efforts would only lead to arguments. So, in time, he found it easier to just convince himself that he really didn't care about her anyway. In so doing, they had fewer tussles, but they also had no love exchanged. As this man and I talked, we came to the conclusion that he was using his "I don't care" attitude to defend himself from his deep feelings of hurt and rejection.

Hiding Out

A more obvious way to be evasively defensive is to hide from the one with whom conflict is likely. The defensive spouse may come to the conclusion that the best way to resist open communication regarding delicate issues is by hiding out, physically keeping one's distance from one's mate. One woman shared with me how she deliberately chose to spend her evenings at home sitting in the bedroom, while her husband stayed in the den. When I asked why she did this, she told me that she just didn't love her husband very much and she really wasn't in the mood to openly address the issue.

Of course, there are other ways spouses can hide out from one another. One mate may be such a workaholic that little time is available for closeness to develop. Another may be so preoccupied in church or civic activities that intimacy is avoided. When hiding out in these various ways becomes a regular routine, it is safe to say that the individual is being defensively resistant to marital interaction.

Being Snobbish

Have you ever thought of snobbish behavior as being defensive? It usually is. The person who has an air of arrogance, who is being snobbish, is usually quite hesitant to be personal with individuals considered to be of "inferior stock." This person closes self off with a "better than thou" attitude, meaning that anything beyond superficial exchanges is avoided. When this occurs within a marriage, the results can be disastrous.

One man shared how he was embarrassed that his wife was talkative and cheerful when they went to social gatherings. She was never inappropriate in her manners, yet she didn't mind letting people in on her little pet peeves, her daily ups and downs, and other personal matters. This husband was appalled that she would actually share bits of her private world with public acquaintances. He had always assumed that no one should ever know his personal feelings or struggles. This problem indicated that his lifestyle was devoted to a closed defensive posture keeping all people, including family, at arm's length. His rationale was that his personal affairs were no one else's business.

Being Lazy

Most lazy people will admit that, when they are in a lazy mood, they tend to be very resistant to any intrusion. When logical reasoning takes hold, they may even admit that *being lazy* is inappropriate behavior. Yet, often they will continue in this habit because, when all things are considered, laziness is what they prefer. In this sense, laziness is seen as a deliberate act of evasive defensiveness. The lazy partner is choosing to sidestep interactions that the spouse might deem important. One lady put it this way: "I know my husband wants me to show more interest in him, but I just don't feel like putting out the effort. I'd rather watch TV." (At least she was honest.)

Laziness is strongly discouraged in the Bible (see Prov. 12:27) because it does little to promote self-improvement or to add to the common good of the family and community. The person who uses this habit frequently is one who is too tuned in to self to be concerned with the work of interpersonal interactions.

Looking over each of the styles of defensiveness listed in this chapter, one thing becomes clear: defensiveness is an easy habit to get into. Most of the tactics listed here are so common that each of us can very easily relate to them. This brings us to the fact that, if defensiveness is to be conquered, we will need a keen awareness of the ease with which we can slip into resistant tactics. This means that concentration in the area of self-awareness is a must.

Also, it is important to recognize that, once these defensive maneuvers are enacted, they tend to create a negative momentum in marital communication. Like any bad habit, when defensiveness is used once, it is easy to repeat it at another time. Eventually, couples can feel like they are stuck in an uncomfortable rut with no way out.

In the next chapter, we will examine how defensive behavior can actually become so habitual that full-blown communication patterns can emerge. It is important to note that, until we are aware of our behavior and habits, our efforts to bring about positive changes will fall short.

4

Defensiveness
Becomes a Habit

Defensiveness rarely isolates itself in communication alone. While we are all complex people in many ways, we also tend to be creatures of habit. And until we make a decision to act differently, most of us will follow predictable patterns of defensive behavior that will continue to bring turmoil into relationships.

Case Example

Terry was known in his family for being hard-headed. Whenever there were personal issues to be discussed, his instinctive response seemed to be to make excuses for himself. He hated to admit errors, and he was highly offended whenever someone would suggest an improvement for him. Because of his high level of defensiveness, over the years Terry developed a pattern of being the boss. Whether it was at home, at work, or even at a party, Terry somehow had to figure a way to be in command. His resistant nature was such that he felt safe only when he was able to place himself above others.

Once individuals latch onto a particular style of communicating, they tend to stay with it. This is why, in my counseling, it is so common for me to hear that individuals who are experiencing marital difficulties have had their problems for years. Even if such a style creates great stress, they persist in using it.

With this in mind, it is important for couples to become aware of the habits they have developed. Only after they become acutely conscious of the problem can there be any success in making the necessary changes to correct it. Spouses need to examine themselves with the goal of gaining an awareness of parts of their communicating practices that can be changed for the better. Now, let's explore some of the more common behavioral patterns that are an extension of a defensive mind-set. As you read through the descriptions, you'll probably be able to relate to more than just one.

Defensive Behavior Patterns

The Chronic Apologizer

Some people are on guard in virtually every act of life. These individuals are all too aware of the fact that they make mistakes or that they may displease others. So, over the course of time, they become prone to apologizing for every minor quirk they have. Usually, by being so apologetic, they only make matters worse for themselves by constantly bringing attention to their faults.

For example, a couple may be entertaining guests in their home and the wife will feel the need to say "I'm sorry" at every turn. As soon as the guests arrive, she says: "Oh, I hope the house isn't too messy, but this has just been one of those disorganized days." When she serves the food she feels compelled to remark: "I'm not sure if the seasoning is right; I hope you'll forgive me." When the kids whine for attention, she says: "I'm sorry the children are in such a bad mood. I just don't know what's gotten into them."

All through the evening she picks up on minor problems and draws attention to them with apologies. In doing so, she is presumably trying to fend off any possibility that someone might question her character. But, in the long run, she succeeds only in making herself feel like a failure.

The Super-friendly Person

In an effort to safeguard themselves from any negative feedback, some defensive people develop a style of life that makes heavy use of the "nice guy" image. These people develop a communication style that overemphasizes the positive, upbeat aspects of their personality. They are quick to show a wide toothy grin. They won't say no, but are exceptionally cooperative even if it means they will have to suffer for it. Whenever they have low or disgruntled moods, they hide their feelings behind a facade of cheerfulness.

When people allow themselves to carry on in this super-friendly fashion, they are usually willing to seek short-term comfort at the expense of long-term discomfort. That is, there is little thought about how a life of surface happiness can actually lead to a dead end of disillusionment. As an illustration, one man who once lived in the super-friendly pattern once shared with me: "On the outside everyone thinks I'm the nicest guy in the world. But inwardly, I'm a wreck. I'd be scared to death to let people know about the insecurities and the anger that's inside me."

In essence, this man had painted himself into a corner. He had worked for so long to build a bubbly, buoyant image that he felt it impossible to allow anyone to see an entirely different side to his personality. Consequently, he felt unbearably guilty whenever a flaw in his outer character would emerge.

The "Lay Low" Personality

Some people are highly skilled in avoiding any controversy or confrontation. While it is normal that they would want to sidestep the discomfort of arguments or disagreements, the "lay low" people take this to the extreme. Being highly skilled in evasive defensive tactics, they not only stay away from disagreeable interactions, but they stay away from virtually any in-depth interchanges. These people are not necessarily shy. In fact, some of them are quite appealing in their social skills. But the key to getting along with them is to keep things shallow. If conversations arise that require deep thought or the sharing of touchy feelings, the "lay low" people can be counted on to duck out of the scene.

What is it that causes such a pattern of communication? Usually we find that, in some way, these individuals have never developed much proficiency in allowing the sensitive side of their personalities to come through. Perhaps they were reared in a home where feelings either were scorned or they weren't talked about. Or maybe they had few friends or little true closeness in the family. Or perhaps a perfectionistic standard was set at home and these people quickly learned to hide anything that hinted at a weakness. Whatever the cause, the "lay low" personalities have developed an entire lifestyle of staying out of anything potentially troubling. This pattern has the advantage of offering the individual comparative peace in life, but it has the disadvantage of guaranteeing little depth or meaning in relationships.

The Constant Critic

It has already been mentioned that some people choose to defend themselves by taking the offense against others. This usually leads to a pattern of being a constant critic. In these people, there is the hidden desire to resist the possibility of being put on the spot or being called to accountability. The way they protect themselves from such worries is to keep the focus on what's wrong with everyone else.

For example, I talked with a man who said that his wife was a huge disappointment to him because she paid too much attention to other family members and not enough was given to him. I asked him if he could shift his mental gears for a moment and describe his idea of how he would like to conduct himself as a husband. His response was that he didn't know how he should act. He was so busy spelling out what was wrong with his wife that it kept him from thinking about how he should behave as a husband! The fact that he kept his mind occupied with criticisms meant that he was "protected" from looking at his own strengths and weaknesses.

When people stay in a pattern of constant criticism, it is usually because there is a need for some diversions to keep themselves from being put on the "hot seat." These individuals are skilled at the game called "Let's Talk About What's Wrong With You." By being judgmental, these people maintain an air of superiority which, in turn, helps fuel the feeling of being beyond the problems of those around them.

The Skeptic

A close cousin to the constant critic is the skeptic. People who fall into this pattern of behaving can usually be overheard saying things like, "I doubt it," or "I can't imagine what would cause you to think that way." These people resist the potential jabs of others by developing a thick-skinned cynicism. Their first reaction to a legitimate feedback is to invalidate the communication as it is being received.

For example, a wife may be reflecting on the instructions given in the pastor's sermon that addresses the issue of gentleness, while her skeptic husband might say something like, "Yeah, he can talk a good game when he's standing in the pulpit, but I wonder what that pastor's really like when he's at home." By choosing to use skepticism, this husband effectively cancels out any validity that might have accompanied the pastor's message. In so doing, he relieves himself from having to act upon the parts of the message that would require self-examination or humbleness.

The skeptic's game is clear: By discounting the importance or validity of another person's thoughts or feelings, they are thereby exonerated from introspection. Since the words of another person carry no meaning for them, they feel no motivation to think matters through. This takes them "off the hook" with regard to any need to change.

The Fuss-budget

When a person has a lifelong habit of communicating from a defensive posture, it is common to find that a pattern of fussiness emerges. True to the definition of defensiveness, the fuss-budget is one who seeks to protect self from the potential discomforts of living. But in doing so, an extreme overemphasis is given to details. These people have such a strong drive to make things right that their minds work overtime to see that everything is in its proper place. Great attention is given to minor, insignificant details, even if it means that relationships suffer.

For example, picture a wife who is finicky to the point of being a regular critic of her husband's dressing habits. In explaining her fussy nature, she says that she is only looking out for the best interests of her husband. But if the truth was known, she would probably be exposed as one who is so defensive regarding her own public reputation that she feels the need to package her entire life perfectly, including the way her husband dresses, so no one can think poorly of her. Her fussy nature indicates the need for perfect acceptance. The true extent of her defensiveness is illustrated when her husband confronts her with the suggestion that she be more accepting of him. This fuss-budget can usually be counted on to sidestep such a confrontation with rationalization or a boomerang response.

People with a finicky, fussy nature need to examine why they *insist* on having things fall properly in place. If they approach the subject with honest objectivity, they will usually uncover an insecure inner core that is uncertain about how to handle close interpersonal interactions. By paying undue attention to unnecessary details, they are excused from the struggle (and vulnerability) that is inherent in intimate exchanges.

The Martyr

On the surface, individuals who adopt the martyr pattern of living would not seem to be defensive in their communications. After all, these people tend to be very open to the duties and obligations of day-to-day living. In fact, many of these people will knock themselves out trying to make positive contributions to relationships. They often are real people-pleasers.

Inherent in the martyr's pattern, though, is a fear of being open and genuine with one's true thoughts and feelings. These people who allow themselves to accept an unfair share of burdens and chores are invariably hesitant to disclose feelings of discomfort or agitation. Preferring to keep the peace at all costs, they will hold their negative feelings inward while outwardly projecting concern and a cooperative spirit. In this sense, they are defending themselves from the struggle that is a natural part of an open, give-and-take communication process.

As an example, imagine the husband who is known by all to be silently cooperative with virtually any request given to him by his wife. Even if the requests are unreasonable or unnecessary, he will comply with her wishes. Though he feels that unfair expectations are being thrust on him insensitively by his wife, he "does his duty" because he has a great dread of what might occur if he ever said no to her. The martyr syndrome is his way of protecting himself from her anger.

The Rebel

In direct contrast to the martyr is the rebel. Individuals who ascribe to this pattern of living are ready to "put up their dukes and fight" at a moment's notice. An "I'll show you" attitude is most prevalent. These people are so resistant to the intrusions of others that a combative pattern of self-protection is the norm. Whenever structure or rules are thrust upon these rebels, they reject them almost instantaneously. Whenever the spouse of a rebel tries to be confrontive (even in a gingerly way) the rebel usually reacts with obvious irritation. Rebels want their partners to know unequivocally that they absolutely, positively, will not be tied down.

It is difficult for a marriage to thrive when one or both of the partners lives with this rebellious pattern. I recall talking with one woman who was so persistently "on edge" that it was extremely difficult to get anywhere with her in conversation. She came to my office complaining that her husband just wasn't sensitive to her. As I would try to speak with her about how to handle such a situation, however, she would quickly butt in saying, "Wait a minute. There's more I have to tell you about my crummy marriage." She would then proceed to spew out all sorts of angry sentiments. This lady needed to recognize that she was so busy responding to her feelings of rebellious resistance to her husband that she was only making matters worse for herself.

The Worrier

Another pattern that frequently emerges from the overuse of defensiveness is the worrier. The people who fall prey to this habit are usually defensive to the extent that there are certain things in their lives that *have to* fall properly in place. Consequently, when these individuals encounter mistakes or variances, they come unglued with a wide variety of frets and fears. For example, a wife who has definitive plans regarding how her husband should conduct himself publicly may worry herself sick thinking about the errors he is likely to make. Or a husband who thinks of his wife as too mistake-prone may drive himself to anguish when she decides to have guests into their home for a social occasion. In each case, these worriers are so consumed with themselves that they mistakenly feel that somehow they can protect their own vested interests by letting anxiety take a foothold in their emotions.

In part, worry can be understood as being a lack of trust. The worrier doesn't trust others to handle responsibilities satisfactorily. Nor does the worrier trust self to have the ability to deal calmly with undesirable circumstances. This lack of trust in self and in others leads to a full-blown pattern of tense defensiveness.

The Legalist

When people have a habit of being defensive, one of the most common resulting patterns is that of becoming a legalist. A legalist is one who relates to life through a strict order of rules and regulations. Fearful of letting themselves act naturally, these people approach responsibilities as if they were dogmatic commandments. Rather than taking the risk of letting themselves be human, these people always do what is right. Their very responsible behavior, however, seems almost machine-like. Their explanation for being right or moral is: "That's what you're *supposed* to do." (They show no indication that they really desire to live right.) One gets the idea that the legalists are too afraid of themselves to let down their guard. It is safer for them to hide behind a wall of duties and regulations because then decisions are automatic. For legalists, thinking is not required, and, consequently, they are not forced to look squarely at their potential limitations.

As an example, think of the wife who has tried to bring predictable structure to virtually every aspect of her life. She works religiously to be prim and proper in her mannerisms. She can be counted on to have dinner on the table precisely as planned. She is very strict with regard to her beliefs about how she and her family should behave. Seemingly, she has her life neatly packaged. But one element is missing. She doesn't allow herself or her family to be human. There is little tolerance for errant emotions or simple mistakes. When a failure occurs, inappropriate guilt follows closely behind. This wife tries to shelter herself with her rules and duties but, in doing so, an aura of stiffness is evident in her home. Neither she nor her family members feel free to drop their guard.

The Emotionally-charged Personality

As defensiveness develops into a full pattern, it is not unusual to find a pattern of emotional tension. That is, people who are regularly defensive will often find themselves displaying a broad array of feelings from anger to worry to depression to envy. It is not unusual for emotional outbursts to occur in defensive people, because their resistant nature is actually an extension of a self-absorbed nature. These people can be much like the husband who would frequently react with undue frustration when his wife said something that he considered inappropriate. This man was so insistent on protecting his ego that he would regularly sulk and pout, and depression and disillusionment were his common companions. He was so tuned in to his needs that he had little control over his emotional reactions.

There is a logical reason why defensive people are easily prone to emotional outbursts. That is, in defensiveness there tends to be a lack of objectivity. The individual is so wrapped up with protecting self that little

66

effort is made to have an open mind toward the communication taking place. Therefore, since objectivity is lacking, the subjective (feeling) side of self takes over. Reactions are quick and emotional, since there is little effort made to put one's objective mind in charge of his or her reactions.

The Boss

Earlier it was mentioned that the best defense may be a good offense. By taking charge of one's environment, it is possible to protect oneself from unwanted intrusions. As long as the other person doesn't have a chance to take the offensive, the defensive person feels safe. Hence, the pattern of bossiness is often chosen by those who are inwardly wishing to ward off potential intrusions. By being in control, the defensive person doesn't have to worry with things like sharing feelings or exposing weaknesses.

The major characteristic that distinguishes the boss is a domineering nature. Usually, whenever a group of people gather together, this person's dominant personality will stand out. A take-charge attitude is evident, as is a strongly opinionated nature. In conversation, people with a bossy personality tend to keep the focus off their own potential weaknesses and onto the chores and obligations that should be followed. They are usually skilled in the boomerang type of defenses. In so doing, they evade personal disclosures.

Although the personality patterns listed in this chapter are quite varied, there is one common characteristic to each one. Each personality pattern is counterproductive to the goal of open, harmonious communications. There is a self-protection mechanism built into each pattern that is unnecessary in normal relations.

Consequently, as you survey these patterns and examine yourself, recognize that, before harmony can be fully achieved, personal habits of resistance will need to be erased. There are many better, more fruitful ways of living than these.

As we continue into the next section, we move to the next aspect of studying defensiveness. That is, we will explore some of the primary emotional and attitudinal factors that cause defensiveness.

Part Two

The Causes
of Defensiveness

5

Fragile Ego:
Handle with Care

"OK, I'll admit it. Sometimes I act defensively. I'd like to change this, but I'm not really sure how to go about it."

These were the words of a man who had sought marriage counseling with his wife, after living through several years of frustrated, bogged-down communication. He and his wife desperately wanted the happiness that they knew marriage could offer. But so far they were stumped in their efforts to achieve it.

I responded, "I think the best place for us to start would be to figure out why this style of behavior occurs in the first place. Understanding yourself will be the necessary initial step. I could very easily tell you what you should do differently, but you won't be as likely to change your communication style until you have a firm comprehension of your inner motives." With that thought, we launched into a series of discussions regarding the various personality factors that led to his resistant manner of interacting. The first factor we explored was his inner feelings of insecurity. As is so often the case, it was apparent that his behavior was indicative of trouble at the "core."

Defensiveness: A Matter of Self-Image

When exploring the issue of why defensive communication exists, we must begin with the question: "What am I defending?" Ultimately, the answer is the same in virtually each case: "I'm defending myself." As mentioned earlier, defensiveness is intricately interwoven with an individual's sense of self-preservation. After all, the most prized possession of each individual is his or her own sense of well-being. In fact, we can assume that virtually all emotional and behavioral reactions are, in some way, a commentary on that person's feeling of worth.

Therefore, since the desire for well-being is such a basic human pursuit, it is only natural that each person would devise various ways to preserve his or her sense of self. Even the Bible tells us in Psalm 8:5 that God has created each person crowned "with glory and majesty." This is why all humans have a natural instinct to protect self. On the inside of each of us is a God-planted notion of personal value. (Because of this, I'm most concerned about people who seem to exhibit no sense of self-preservation.) No wonder we tend to defend ourselves in the face of a perceived threat! We are attempting to keep self from any drudgery or sense of ill feeling that we assume we don't deserve.

But here's the catch. People who feel the need to defend themselves very often or very strongly are indicating a *lack* of any true feeling of self-worth. By resorting to defensive tactics to the extent that they are always going to bat for self, defensive people are, in essence, communicating: "I feel weak. I'm afraid of breaking. I'm so needy of positive input that I can't bear the thought of having to struggle with personal discomforts." By throwing up their guards too often, defensive people show that they are living as if they are completely out of touch with their God-given sense of self-worth. So fragile are they that nothing can be allowed in their lives that might rock the boat. These people may not be consciously aware that their behavior communicates this lack of a feeling of self-confidence. Yet we assume that the best way to get a good measure of one's inner feelings about self is to observe outward behaviors.

Case Example

Paula was a very controlled person who prided herself in being able to speak and behave properly in social circumstances. She was the kind of person who was so firm in her sense of etiquette that she was readily critical of people who were uncouth or unrefined. While she tended to be a closed person anyway, there was one thing that could cause Paula to become especially defensive. That is, she became highly sensitive whenever anyone would question her style of handling interpersonal matters.

For example, if her husband ever shared a thought about how she might consider a more flexible approach to handling her grievances with her in-laws, she would instantly recoil. She always had an explanation for her set ways of doing things and she resented the very idea that her husband would even question her. Or if a friend would ever probe her in hopes of learning how Paula handled personal problems, she would give a superficial answer and cleverly change the subject. (She assumed that her personal matters were no one else's business.)

On the outside, Paula seemed to be the perfect picture of composure and self-confidence. Yet her ready defensive nature told another story. Her defensiveness communicated that inwardly she was afraid to be vulnerable, to take the risk of exposing a weakness, or to admit an error. By *having* to appear above the problems of common people, Paula illustrated a serious problem in the area of her true feelings of self-worth.

You see, a large percentage of people have not been adequately trained to know how to mentally grasp the notion of their God-given sense of self-worth. Most people have grown up assuming that their worthiness was determined by their ability to prove it in outward ways. Rather than being taught to maintain a positive self-image based on one's inner notions of God's love, most people learn to feel positively about themselves based on external factors such as their performance in life and proper emotional control.

During their formative years, few people had someone talk with them regularly regarding how to understand their God-given sense of value. Many people are told, as children, what to do or what not to do in interpersonal relations and social situations, in an attempt to establish a sense of their value in the minds of other people. But that's not the same as discussing the matter of our unconditional worth. This helps explain why most people grow up with a sense of self-worth that is determined by external factors, instead of inner beliefs. This type of conditioning makes them more prone to defensiveness, because it teaches them to be too sensitive to the words and feelings of others. So, in a sense, we can say that defensive people behave the way they do because they have learned to be highly sensitive to the opinions of the people around them, rather than learning to hold firmly to the inner value given each person by God himself.

As a person becomes more deeply entrenched in a defensive pattern, certain indicators usually emerge that point to trouble in the realm of self-image. To break the defensive pattern then, it would be prudent for that individual to examine those indicators in order to reevaluate the foundation stones of his or her inner feelings about self. Let's examine some of these factors that are associated with a low sense of self-worth.

Overemphasis on Personal Needs

God has placed within all of us the capacity and desire to care for ourselves. This is manifested in our most basic instincts, such as seeking food and seeking love. Likewise, this inborn desire to care for ourselves is displayed in our emotions. For example, if we had no inner drive for personal safekeeping, we would never become frustrated or annoyed. The person who feels such emotions is assuming that life should have more to offer than uncalled-for disturbances. So, it is normal for an individual to have reactions that are intended to keep him/herself comfortable.

As is the case with so many positive matters, however, this desire to care for oneself can become so exaggerated that it can become a negative trait. A person who places too much emphasis on meeting his or her own personal needs is turning something useful into something negative. As an analogy, imagine a person who feels compelled to eat six large meals per day rather than the standard of three balanced ones. The overeater is abusing the natural need for nourishment. He or she is turning something positive—eating—into something negative.

Such is the case with the chronically defensive person. This person has such a strong emphasis on self that it is abnormal. The defensive person is concerned with self-protection (which is fine), but it is displayed so often or so powerfully that it becomes negative, since it creates sour moods and detracts from the harmony desired for us by God.

It is interesting to note that people can be very easily trained to become self-absorbed. For example, I've spoken with many men and women who could trace their defensiveness back to childhood days when they were taught to be afraid of making mistakes. Being in an atmosphere that was unaccepting of personal weaknesses, these people learned at an early age to be highly self-conscious. Consequently, they would carry this same tendency into their marriages and other adult relations.

In addition, I've heard men and women speak about how they would spend their work days under the control of an extremely scrutinous boss. Being in such an environment, these people learn to be wary of their actions. Fearing the loss of their jobs, they learn defensiveness as a way of life. Again, it is predictable that such a pattern of self-focus can be carried home. People can easily be drawn into patterns of self-absorption, barely aware that such behavior is occurring.

Case Example

Mike admits that he had always been extremely self-conscious. He says that he can recall how he would recoil, during his boyhood days, whenever his parents, teachers, or friends would suggest that he had made a mistake. For as long as he could remember, it had never been excusable for him to err. Consequently, he developed a self-conscious nature that was often so strong that he had tremendous struggles throughout his early years trying to maintain the proper outer image. You can imagine that, once he became married, he continued in this problem. Just as he had done when he was younger, he would snap back quickly whenever his wife seemed to be questioning him. He did this so frequently that she began feeling unappreciated and lonely.

In counseling, I had the chance to ask Mike how his defensive behaviors related to his self-image. Quite candidly he responded, "I don't think I've ever admitted this to anyone, but the truth is that I start feeling really insecure whenever someone even hints that they disagree with me. I guess you might say that I've been so worried all my life with my need to protect my respectability that it's really become a bad habit." Only after admitting his insecurity and strong self-focus was Mike able to make real headway in relationships with his wife and family members.

As was the case with Mike, most defensive people have such a strong focus on self that their resistant behaviors are a dead giveaway for a weak feeling inwardly. The stronger one's sense of protest becomes, the more it illustrates insecure worry about self.

Fear of Being Vulnerable

When a person has a communication pattern that indicates a feeling of weakness at the core of the personality, it is logical to assume that he or she is operating according to a deep fear of being personally vulnerable. To be vulnerable means to be in a potential position to be hurt or to feel unmasked. It means that there is a susceptibility to possible attacks and subsequent exposure of inadequacies. Therefore, a person who is fearful of being personally vulnerable is assuming that the risk of letting people see his/her inner flaws would come at too great a cost. There is an implied notion that one would collapse psychologically if attacked.

Now, obviously, no sane person would deliberately invite personal discomfort. Yet, it is safe to say that a secure, confident person is not going to feel compelled to hide behind a thick wall of defense whenever a challenge arises. When a person has a sound comprehension of personal worth, he or she knows that it will not suddenly disappear if a flaw is exposed. In humbleness, the secure person is willing to admit his or her imperfections without fear of a lowered personal standing. The defensive person, on the other hand, can have a feeling of near paranoia that vulnerability would surely spell doom for self. This person's confidence is so fragile that there is an inability or unwillingness to withstand the stress of being questioned.

Second Timothy 1:7 reads: "For God has not given us a spirit of timidity, but of power and love and discipline." From this verse, we can stand firmly on the notion that while none of us may relish the idea of being "put to trial," neither should we become consumed with fear when personal trials arise. We are promised that God can empower us with the means to withstand moments of tension. In practical terms, this means that spouses need not cringe when flaws are discussed, because they can hold to the confidence that solutions are available.

At this point, it is necessary to note that most defensive people won't admit that their behavior is motivated by fear. By definition, these individuals hesitate to acknowledge anything that sheds a negative light on self. And admitting fears is not flattering. Consequently, it would be common to hear a defensive person say: "It's not that

I'm afraid of being vulnerable; I just don't feel like telling the whole world about my inner feelings." Yet we know that having a closed communication style is counter to God's plan for marital relations (see Gal. 6:2). Therefore, it is only natural to assume that fear is involved in some way. Notice how fear was behind the defensive behavior in the following situation.

Case Example

Curtis shared with me how he had lived for years with a secret that tormented him so much that he would readily turn himself off from intimate conversations with his wife. In his early adult years, he had become involved in alcohol and drug abuse, which had led to a life-style of risk and suspense. However, his way of life eventually caught up with him. He was arrested for both the possession and selling of an illegal drug. Because of this, he had spent several months in a prison and, forevermore, he was to be branded an ex-con.

After this experience, he met and married his wife. He made the decision to turn his life over to the Lord and became committed to a wholesome lifestyle. Consequently, he felt no need to ever talk about the experiences of his past with anyone, including his wife. On the surface, he rationalized this by saying that it was best to just let the past lay. But truthfully, he was ashamed of himself and he feared that he would be quickly rejected if his past mistakes were known.

Because of the fear of being found out, Curtis would go to extreme measures to avoid all conversations about his own past or about someone else's problems. He was assuming that, by keeping things to himself, he could assure himself of less inner pressure. However, Curtis shared with me that, as the years had gone by, it was actually more difficult for him to feel comfortable with himself and, consequently, with his wife. Deep down he felt like a phony.

As I talked with him, I suggested that he might relieve his burden if he would share some of his unflattering experiences with his wife. It was a calculated risk and he wasn't sure how she would respond, but he decided to give it a try. When he shared his drug experiences with his wife, she responded in love and understanding: "I knew you weren't an angel before we met, but your past doesn't bother me. I decided a long time ago to accept you for who you are." Because he had not known how his wife would react, Curtis was overjoyed by her re-assurances. By making himself vulnerable, he took a risk, but he also succeeded in allaying a great fear that had plagued him all his married life. Knowing that he didn't need to fear his wife's rejection, he felt as if a ton of bricks had fallen off his back.

Most people don't have extreme experiences like Curtis's that they keep locked away in their secret closets. Yet each of us has had some humbling experience that we prefer to keep to ourselves. By holding these experiences inward, we are depriving others of the chance to relate to us on a human, real level. By opening self up through discreet sharing, we could bring a greater depth to our relationships. While it would not be wise to proclaim all flaws to all people, most of us would find that having an openness regarding weaknesses is not as devastating as we might imagine. Becoming vulnerable is an offshoot of feeling confident. Hiding one's real self is an indication of a mind-set of fear and intimidation.

A Reactor Mentality

Defensive people are reactors (as opposed to being initiators). Their moods and behaviors hinge on the words and feelings of the people around them. If they are treated with kindness and respect, defensive people can be expected to react with a calm mood and a pleasant demeanor. But if they perceive that they are not being given proper treatment, their moods can instantly turn sour or resistant. Rather than thinking about how to create a mood conducive to harmony, these people are busy responding with knee-jerk reflexes to the world around them. Little effort is made by the defensive person to set one's mind on positive, constructive thoughts and feelings.

When a person has a habit of letting his or her moods hinge on the actions of surrounding people, it is a signal that there are problems in that person's self-image. Very subtly, the reactor is paying self an insult. In essence, by behaving resistantly due to another person's actions, this behavior communicates: "I won't be able to act patiently or harmoniously until my circumstances are to my liking. I don't have the ability to be cooperative if things don't go exactly right."

By letting the moods of another person govern self, the defensive person assumes a position of helplessness in the area of personal relationships. The implied message is: "How can I be pleasant if you aren't?"

Being a reactor, in and of itself, is not necessarily a negative characteristic; not at all. It is very natural for a person to be sensitive to the words and feelings of others to the extent that one's own feelings are influenced. For example, most of us would react with warm feelings if we were to see a child playing happily with a puppy. Or we would react with negative feelings if someone were to speak slanderously about a close friend. But here is the problem: Defensive people tend to react so often or powerfully to uncomfortable circumstances that they seem to lose the ability to contribute in a positive way to relationships. Their tendency to react is so strong that negative, unwanted emotions (such as stubbornness or pride) take over. One's sense of fair play and objective sensitivity is lost.

Case Example

Molly openly admitted to me that she was a stubborn, inflexible person. She said that she didn't particularly want to be that way but, seemingly, she had no choice, because her husband didn't communicate with her in the way she wanted. She thought she could be more cooperative in her communication if he would just learn to be a better communicator. I said to her, "If that's the case, you may have a long wait before you change. I wonder if you would go ahead and become a harmonizer, even in spite of his style." She responded quickly, "No, I don't think that would work. I have to have positive signs first from him in order to have better communication." With that thought it was clear that Molly would continue to experience frustrating and resistant feelings in her marriage. She was assuming an inability to get her own house in order as long as her husband was imperfect.

A Need for Power

Another ego issue at the heart of defensive behavior is the desire for power. In essence, whenever a person becomes involved in defensive behavior, that person is also becoming involved in a power struggle. The defensive person is acting on the need to be in control of his or her immediate surroundings, so much so that unnecessary effort is made to gain the upper hand over one's partner. The defensive person usually feels put down or cornered when the resistant behavior occurs, and it is usually quite clear that the person resorts to defensive tactics as a means of gaining superiority. This explains why a husband may remain silent to his wife's pleading for better communication. By using such a tactic, he is remaining above the problem at hand. Likewise, if a wife snaps defensively at her husband's request for a quicker dinner, she is seeking to "put him in his place," while elevating herself to a position of being beyond his approach. These are power tactics that serve the purpose of allowing a spouse to have his or her own way in the marriage relationship.

In many cases, it seems strange to assume that a marital "power broker" is one who suffers from a fragile ego. After all, these people are often quite skilled in the ability to outwardly exude such traits as confidence, composure, and decisiveness. But the fact that there is a defensive reaction to personal or emotionally-charged issues is an indication that this strong front may be merely a facade for feelings of insecurity. People who need to maintain tight control in their relationships are people who have a deflated sense of confidence with regard to their abilities to handle the nitty-gritty of personal imperfections.

As is the case with the people who have a fear of vulnerability, the people who are very controlled in their relationships are prone to rationalizing their behavior by saying, "Why should I share my gut-level feelings with my spouse? What good would it do?" There is a tendency to shy away from personal sharing, not because it is useless (although they may give this reason), but because they fear their hold or influence over their spouse might decrease if a personal inadequacy is revealed. In a sense, it may be assumed that such people need power in order to feel positive about themselves. It is a sort of "fix" that keeps them feeling superior.

Case Example

Phil was a high-powered attorney who was extremely successful in his field because he had learned years ago how to play his cards in such a way that others were kept on their toes. He was skilled in winning by intimidation. He knew how to be a master controller and he found that it brought him respect and acclaim.

However, Phil had a very unsettled marital life. While his power tactics worked well in business, he found they failed miserably at home. He stayed in a chronic state of frustration with his wife, because she was not one who took kindly to his bossy and overbearing ways. Whenever she would sit down with him to talk out their problems, he was careful never to admit a failing, because that would cause him to lose his power base. Likewise, he was stubborn in his insistence that his wife should behave just as he prescribed. But he found that this only fueled her annoyances with him. His style of being powerful at work may have brought him success in that realm, but Phil needed to understand that such tactics were not conducive to a successful marriage.

Summary

It is clear that people who resort to frequent defensive tactics live according to the assumption that personal weaknesses or interpersonal struggles indicate failure. The fact that large amounts of energy are expended to avoid such struggles is an indication of a deep feeling of inability to handle such matters. By trying to avoid the tensions of marital interaction, defensive people are giving themselves a stamp of no confidence.

Also, the people who protect their egos by unnecessary

defensiveness are prone to thinking in unrealistic, idealistic terms regarding their marriage. There is an implied assumption that everything can and should go smoothly, if only the rules are followed properly. There seems to be an inability on the part of defensive people to adjust to the blemishes in relationships. Again, this is all a part of an excessive need to protect self from tensions and worries.

6

Good Is
Never Good Enough

In the last chapter, we asked the question, "What is it that a defensive person is defending?" We answered that a person is defending self. In this chapter, we will explore the question, "What am I defending myself against?" We will explore how, in a majority of cases, the resistant person is defending self from the judgments of others.

No one likes to be judged. Most of us would agree that relationships lose their appeal when a heavy cloud of criticism and evaluation hangs constantly overhead. One woman shared her sentiments with me by saying, "I feel like my husband expects me to jump through hoops like a trained animal before he will pay me compliments. I hate feeling like I'm supposed to perform for him before he will show any acceptance of me." As you could easily imagine, this woman struggled frequently with defensive communications due to the mandate that she had to perform.

Defensive people are prompted to act in the resistant

way because they are highly sensitive to the judgments that are a sure (or assumed) part of their relationships. Conditioned by years of being graded and scrutinized, defensive people have learned to be cautious in their words and actions. Their defensive behavior implies a wariness and an intolerance of constant feeling of being "sized up." This feeling can be so strong that they can feel an aversion even when a partner tells them how good they are. Even the label *good* can have negative connotations to defensive people, because it can make them feel compelled to perform "properly," merely to maintain that good status.

Case Example

Keith admitted to me that he had a jumpy, sensitive nature. He was quickly defensive whenever his wife asked questions (however innocently) regarding his daily schedule. In addition, he didn't enjoy his children because he felt inadequate in knowing how to communicate with them on their level. Consequently, he projected a leave-me-alone attitude toward them at home. In his job, he was insecure because his boss would never let him know where he stood. He had to play a constant guessing game regarding his status among his colleagues. It seemed that, in the most important aspects of his life, Keith was ultra-sensitive to the point of not being able to really enjoy his closest relationships.

As we explored the reasons for his touchy nature, we quickly focused on the fact that this problem had been with him since boyhood. He had a strict dad who seemed more prone to pointing out what Keith did wrong than commenting on what he did right. And even when Keith did get a compliment from him, he still felt uncertain, because he knew he would eventually show a weakness that would quickly erase his favorable status. He was an exceptional student but, in spite of his high marks, he never felt like he could make good-enough grades. Whenever he made a 95 on a test, he worried that he should have scored 100. Furthermore, with his peers, Keith had learned to be highly conscientious regarding his social prowess. He was never quite sure if he measured up to the standard that would keep him with the "in crowd."

The more Keith shared his background with me, the more evident it was that he suffered from the problem of feeling judged at every turn. It was clear that he needed to learn to separate himself from human judgments, so that he could move forward in his efforts to have a more comfortable, secure style of communicating.

Shakespeare was correct when he wrote "All the world's a stage." From earliest childhood through latest adulthood, we have the eyes of our family and friends upon us, watching our every move, making regular evaluations of our performances. It is a certainty that, as long as we have personal interactions, we will receive judgments. And while those judgments tend to revolve around external factors, most of us tend to internalize them, basing our feelings about self on those judgments. We tend to place great prominence on the evaluations received from others. And, in doing so, we can become defensive to the point that it alters our ability to follow guidelines for harmonious interactions.

Items on Your "Report Card"

Given the fact that judgments can create a feeling of inner tension, it is no wonder that defensiveness follows. After years of exposure to endless grading systems, men and women learn to behave in ways that will presumably shelter them from a barrage of judgments. We can be like the husband who learned quickly that his wife thought he was "neat" if he exhibited certain traits like friendliness and gentleness. This man figured that the best way to keep harmony at home was to play up to her preferences, even if it meant being phony.

However, as you might guess, this man was also keenly aware of the behaviors his wife frowned on, meaning that he learned to cover up (as best he could) the aspects of his personality that would arouse her criticisms. In the short term, he was able to keep himself out of hot water and in her good graces. But as the years went by, a growing distance developed in their relationship because of his need to hide parts of himself from her.

Think about your interactions with others. You know that every day you live you will be graded, evaluated, or judged in some way. This may occur quite openly or it may be present silently. For the most part, a few judgments here and there won't cause us much distress. But when these judgments are numerous, they can be very disturbing, leading to a strong defensive nature. Let's examine some of the common judgments we each tend to be exposed to.

Judgments in Task Performance

Notice how we tend to speak to each other when we accomplish our routine chores. We usually find it necessary to make an evaluation statement regarding the "okay–ness" of our performance:

"I don't think you're behaving like a good husband should."

"I think the meal would have been better if you had used a little less salt."

"You've got to get the yard looking good because we're having company this weekend."

"Don't you have something better to wear?"

"You need to improve in the way you talk to our neighbors."

"You're not friendly enough."

Even though there are more personable ways to speak with one another (which we'll discuss in the next few pages), most of us seem habitually to make evaluative statements whenever we notice the actions of others. Seemingly, when these statements are examined one at a time, they are relatively harmless. And yet, they can bring tension to a person who dislikes being heavily scrutinized in virtually all aspects of performing. Evaluative statements can be spoken so freely that spouses can become very sensitive regarding the ways they are being perceived. We like to receive evaluations such as "excellent," "great," or "outstanding," but we cringe at the thought of being graded as "unreliable," "no good," or "inept." Some people put so much emphasis on these evaluations (either consciously or subconsciously) that they arrange their entire communication style in order to gain only positive judgments.

Case Example

Patti came to my office stating that she had a serious problem in being open and honest with her husband. She said that she frequently would play up to her husband, telling him whatever she thought he wanted to hear. And she would also hide facts about herself that she thought her husband would find unflattering. I asked her if she had any idea why she did this. She responded quickly with, "Oh, yes. The reason I have this style of communication is due to the fact that I live in fear of how he might perceive me. But then, I guess I've had this problem ever since I was a girl." As we went on in our discussions, it became quite clear to Patti that her defensive style of marital interaction was directly attributable to the fact that she readily responded to any grade or evaluation given to her by someone else. Her entire self-image was wrapped up in her performance standards.

Try to recall the number of times in your life that your performances have been evaluated. Actually, you can't. It would be impossible. We each have been graded many, many times in the way we speak, the way we dress, the way we perform in competitions, the way we fulfill requirements, the way we handle ourselves socially. Each single judgment by itself seems harmless. But when we add them all together into one big cluster, we can began to understand why so many of us get to the point of dodging those judgments as if they were bullets! We tend to develop a built-in resistance to the idea of having to perform first for positive recognition.

Emotional Judgments

In addition to being judged for our performances, most of us have had the experience of being graded for the emotions we feel. We know, for instance, that people will label us as good if we feel happy and bad if we feel up-tight. Early in life most of us learned that certain emotions were acceptable while others were not. As an example, notice how we adults have an instinctive tendency to shame a child when he or she admits to having feelings of hate. We instantly let the child know that such feelings won't be tolerated. The child then readily assumes the evaluation of being a "bad kid." But notice what this leads to. The child doesn't necessarily stop feeling hate. In fact, after assuming the label of bad, he or she may become *more* entrenched in the feeling of hate. Knowing the parent will display scorn whenever hate is displayed, the child merely learns to hide this emotion behind the parent's back. The child's problem of hate is not resolved when a judgment is placed on him or her. Rather, the troubles are enhanced because the new dimension of defensiveness is added to the feeling of hate.

Go through a list of emotions and notice how we will pronounce some as good and some as bad. (Note that when we do this, it usually follows that we are in danger of labeling the person feeling those emotions as either good or bad.) In the good category we would list joy, contentment, love, and peace. And in the bad category, we would list such feelings as envy, anger, anxiety, and impatience. Notice that, while we find the Bible has quite a bit to say about the appropriateness and inappropriateness of various emotions, it stops short of suggesting that we should label each other according to the emotions we feel. A person's God-given worth does not go up or down whenever that person feels a "good" emotion or a "bad" emotion. Yet many people have a hard time experiencing an emotion or witnessing someone else's emotion without also assuming a judgment.

This all points to the idea that there is a very fine distinction between feeling an appropriate or inappropriate emotion and being labeled as a bad or good person. No human being has been given the right by God to judge another person based on the emotions felt by that individual. God knows that no individual has the sufficient ability to discern what any human's ultimate judgment should be. He wants us to learn the difference between right and wrong, helpful and harmful. But he wants us to stay out of the business of being judges of one another's worth. That is why he has asked us, in Matthew 7:1, to "judge not."

Rather than giving one another judgments according to the emotions of the moment, we would be wiser stewards of our time if we would attempt to do two things:

1. Try to show understanding to one another whenever emotions are expressed. Even when harsh feelings are felt, seek to understand that person's inner struggles.
2. Work to monitor our own emotions, based on sound biblical teachings.

Couples would find far less defensiveness in their communications if they expended their energies in these efforts rather than in the trading of value judgments.

Religious Judgments

Those of us who have been exposed to religious teachings have heard many discussions regarding right and wrong ways to live. For instance, virtually all of us know that mature Christians will exhibit patience and kindness, have a willingness and desire to be open in their witness, and make regular efforts to stay close to the Lord in prayer and Bible study. We know what it takes to attain the label "good Christian."

And yet, we must each ask, "Who am I to say who is a good Christian and who is not?" Since I don't possess the wisdom of God, I don't have the right to put a grade on anyone. (I may be able to discern what is pleasing to God and what is not, but that is different from giving an evaluation.) God has given each of us two major responsibilities regarding Christian maturity: (1) to seek to have a thorough understanding of his Word in order to live according to God's desires, and (2) to live in such a way that our life is a witness and testimony to others who are also seeking to know God. We must remind ourselves that he has given no human the position of judge.

Many times I have talked with a husband and wife who are experiencing defensive communications because one (or perhaps both) feels unable to live up to the religious standards of the spouse. For example, many wives will say: "My husband wants me to be submissive like the Bible says, but I don't think I can live up to his expectations." Or a husband may explain, "Every time I go home I feel like I'm condemned if I don't exhibit the fruit of the Spirit in exactly the way my wife prescribes it." In other words, we can become so dogmatic in our religious beliefs that a judgmental, defensive atmosphere can easily grow in the home. When this occurs, we are missing the point of God's teachings.

God never intended to spell out the rules of right and wrong behavior so that husbands and wives could have "ammunition" to shoot at each other in order to gain each other's "good" behavior. And he didn't give us the teachings about correct living so that we could have legitimate grounds from which to argue our personal ambitions and preferences. Rather, God has given us biblical teachings on order that we each might be prompted to search ourselves in order to discover our continuing need to find God's will for our personal lives. The Bible was never meant to be a rule book that prompts a judgmental nature.

The Replacement for Judgments

One conclusion should be clear: If judgments and evaluations abound in a marriage, a well-ingrained pattern of defensiveness will surely follow. There is no room for an attitude of criticism in any marriage that is seeking biblically-oriented harmony.

With this thought in mind, let's examine a couple of alternatives to judgments.

Examine Rather than Criticize

A woman once asked me: "If I am going to refrain from judgments in my marriage, does that mean I'll just abandon my beliefs about good and bad?" I assured her that need not be the case. "It's possible for you to continue to hold your beliefs about what is good and bad without making a judgment of a person's innate value." As an example, I mentioned to her how we can correct the improper behavior of our children without making any reference to the child's worth. We might say something like, "I'd rather that you not play with the tools in the garage; you can play with your toys in the yard instead." Right principles can be taught without placing a grade on the child's performance.

Obviously, in any marriage, husbands and wives will have reasons to discuss thoughts and feelings about proper versus improper matters. When this is done, it is possible that the couple can objectively examine each other's deeds and emotions without an attitude of judgment. It's delicate, but it is definitely possible! Notice how the couple in the following illustration did this.

Case Example

Bob and Barbara had just experienced one of those days when they just didn't seem to click in their interactions. That is, Bob had been in a somewhat impatient mood and Barbara wasn't exactly tolerant of him. Consequently, she was fussy and he was edgy most of the day. Before they sat down for dinner, Bob suggested that they discuss their foul moods. Bob began: "It looks like this day just hasn't gone well for us. Neither one of us has been in the most cooperative spirit. Do you suppose that it's possible for us to salvage the evening?" Barbara was quick to agree and she responded: "I'd really like to do something different because I know that we haven't been very successful so far in having a pleasant day." With that, they each admitted how there had been an insensitivity in their interactions. And they each spelled out suggestions that would lead to a more satisfying evening. Nothing was said about who was at fault, but there was an honest exchange regarding what each didn't like about the day and what needed to be changed. After about ten minutes, they ended the discussion in agreement to pursue harmony.

When examining behaviors and communications, couples will be seeking to gain a fair and objective appraisal of the subject before them. For example, a husband and wife can discuss why they feel angry without resorting to name-calling or blaming. In addition, couples can share their needs with each other without making each other feel guilty or on the spot. Clear, constructive discussions can occur when couples jointly decide to examine their needs and differences with an open mind, with no intent to corner each other.

In order to shift from a judging style of communication to an examining style of communication, two key factors are necessary:

1. Listening that is pursued in earnest. Each spouse will make a diligent effort to be certain that the other's thoughts and feelings are comprehended. Even if the spouses don't agree with each other, an all-out effort can be made to see things from the other's point of view. Listening is crucial to the examining style of communications.

2. Tact and diplomacy used in speaking. When a person has a judgmental mindset, the goal of communication is guilt induction and manipulation. But when a person has an examining mindset, the goal of communication is a clear, yet considerate exchange of thoughts and feelings. As couples examine their thoughts and feelings, they have a genuine desire to bring their conversations to a constructive end. And they know that the best way to have har-

mony is to speak in a manner that ascribes worth and value to each other.

Be Descriptive Rather than Evaluative

As a further means of keeping judgments at a minimum, it is possible for couples to share their opinions with each other in a descriptive rather than in an evaluative way. In virtually any conversation in which an opinion is expressed, it is possible to refrain from words that denote judgments of good or bad, using words that are more neutral in their meaning instead. As an example, look at the following two statements and decide which one you would rather hear.

1. "I never thought you would ever stoop to the position of yelling at me. Where's your self-respect? Don't you know how wrong you are?" (The implied message is, "You sure are a bad spouse.") Or,
2. "I'd like to try to understand what you are feeling. I think I'd feel more comfortable if we could speak tactfully with each other. I'm willing if you are." (No evaluation about the spouse's worth is given. Instead, a description of one's desires is given.)

Descriptive speech seeks to sidestep the issue of how good or how bad a person is. The spouse who utilizes this style of speaking has no desire to place self in a superior position over the spouse, making judgments about that person's actions. Rather, one's focus is on presenting one's ideas in as constructive a manner as possible. The focus is on the exchange of facts and ideas that are a part of building a coherent understanding of one another.

Couples who wish to exchange thoughts and feelings constructively will remind themselves that their words will have a great impact when they are conveyed within an attitude of respect. The most precious gift that one spouse can give to the other is an acknowledgment of the other's value. We each need to know that our closest companion is one who views us as someone significant. This is why descriptive communication is far more desirable than evaluative. Evaluative words give others the impression of having to meet a standard before respect is given. Descriptive words imply that others are considered already worthy of proper treatment.

In addition, evaluative discussions tend to limit the scope of conversations, whereas descriptive exchanges encourage deeper communication. For instance, when a husband and wife merely speak to each other regarding what they are supposed to do to gain each other's approval, they can become easily hung up on how good or how mediocre they each may be. But if the husband and wife will share feelings, perceptions, and beliefs, their communication takes on depth. They are not as consumed with mere window dressing as they are with understanding each other's innermost person.

Case Example

Leonard and Melissa had struggled for years in a "one-up, one-down" game. That is, there seemed to be a continual competition between them to see who could gain the upper hand when decisions were to be made. As a result, heavy uses of judgmental message were made. They poured their emotional energies into efforts to prove self as good and the other as "not so bright." Naturally, there was a heavy cloud of tension in their home most of the time.

But as the years went by and as their feelings of frustration rose, this couple came to the conclusion that changes needed to be made. When they came into my counseling office, Leonard told me, "We'd really like to do something different in our marriage. Something is not working right and we need to discover what to do."

As I came to know this couple, their tendency toward evaluative communication became glaringly apparent. As we focused on this problem, we practiced over and over the skills involved in descriptive communication. They each learned to share their feelings in a straightforward manner, with no intent to place guilt on the other. In addition, they took some of the coerciveness and condemnation out of their tone of voice, replacing it with gentleness and "matter-of-fact" speech.

They each came to the conclusion that it simply was not their place to hold the other in judgment. Besides, by instigating a system of communication that emphasized the sharing of thoughts and feelings in a descriptive fashion, they found a whole new realm of understanding and acceptance.

Romans 15:7 tells us, "Accept one another, just as Christ also accepted us to the glory of God." We are not required to prove ourselves as worthy in thought and deed before we can receive the love of God. Therefore, since we are accepted by God without condemnation when we become a part of his family, it would be consistent for us to seek this same attitude in our earthly families.

7

But I Insist!

In the last two chapters, we discussed how defensiveness can stem from a fragile ego and an atmosphere of judgment. In this chapter we will explore another factor in the making of a defensive nature—the insistent mindset.

There is a major problem that consistently leads to stalemates in marital communication, creating a defensive atmosphere. That problem is the problem of being right. There are times when spouses feel so right about certain issues that their beliefs and opinions become a detriment to marital harmony. Marriage partners can feel so sure about their thoughts and preferences that a destructive, insistent style of behavior erupts. One man who recognized this tendency in himself put it this way: "There are times when I'm so right that I'm wrong." It seems strange to think that a person can have such a firm clasp on what is correct that the person suffers as a result. Yet it happens frequently.

Invariably, defensive spouses have difficulties in knowing how to be right. It's not at all unusual to witness a mate who knows that he or she is right on an issue and who then develops a style of relating that utilizes such traits as a critical demeanor, stubbornness, or a derogatory style of speech. That person can be so committed to his or her own opinions that there is a blindness or even an indifference to the negative behaviors that follow. When this happens, being correct (as opposed to being harmonious) is the defensive person's number one goal. Even though the stubborn spouse may be aware that the marital relationship is being damaged, there is a persistent holding on to one's belief. When this occurs, the marital partner can bear a close resemblance to the Pharisees of biblical days who held firmly to their long list of rules and regulations to such an extent that they were out of touch with the needs and feelings of the individuals around them.

Think about a recent time when you became defensive. Perhaps you can remember a time when you snapped at your spouse who had just mentioned that it was time to get ready and go somewhere. Or maybe you can recall a time when you gave your mate the silent treatment during a tense and delicate discussion. What were you trying to communicate by being defensive? As you analyze your behavior, you will probably find that the defensive was an offshoot of an insistent mind-set.

For example, the spouse who snaps back at being told that it's time to go somewhere may be inwardly thinking, "There's no reason why my mate should be so pushy whenever we have some place to go. I'm not about to take kindly to such rudeness." This person would be holding insistently to the opinion that it is just not right to be bossed by one's mate. Yet no matter how justifiable that position may be, the snappy behavior is still inappropriate. The problem here is that the defensive mate is too busy using his or her energies toward self-justification to acknowledge the inappropriateness of the communication style.

There are many different issues among spouses in which an insistent style of thinking can occur. Yet there are also some very common opinions that spouses are likely to cling to fervently. Some of these are:

"My spouse had better speak to me at all times in a pleasant tone of voice."

"You'd better be in a good mood today, because you've been cranky all week."

"I get tired of the way you question me. You ought to be more agreeable."

"Just leave me alone and let me do things my way."

"It doesn't make sense that you're so emotional. You're going to have to learn how to be calm."

"I just wish that my mate would be more understanding. It's ridiculous how he (or she) just doesn't make the effort to comprehend my feelings."

"Why won't you talk? We can't have good communication if you just sit there!"

"I'm not going to take it if my spouse speaks unkindly to me. He (or she) is just going to learn that rude talking doesn't work."

Technically speaking, each of the sentiments expresed above are correct. In each of the thoughts mentioned, we could make a strong case regarding why a person would legitimately think that way. Yet we still must hold firmly to the notion that having correct opinions does not give a person the right to respond negatively.

In order to properly control the tendency to have an insistent style of thinking, we will want to hold on to a major concept: *Right is not always the ultimate issue.* As good as it is to have proper opinions, there is a higher level of thinking to be sought. That higher level of thought seeks to answer the question, "How can I be most loving?"

In other words, love has a higher priority over being right. This thought is in accordance with 1 Corinthians 13:3 which states, if I "do not have love, it profits me nothing."

Case Example

"I'm sorry if I act stubborn with my wife, but I just can't help it. My wife just has a way of talking negatively that is clearly wrong!" Will was expressing his long-held frustrations that he had experienced in his marital communications. And in truth, he really did have some legitimate reasons for his feelings. Will was committed to bringing harmony to his relationship with his wife, but he felt stymied whenever she would speak critically or fuss at him unnecessarily. Whenever she would speak to him in an unbecoming way, he would almost instinctively recoil in his emotions. Frequently, he would snap at her, insisting that she shouldn't talk to him in a negative way. At other times, he would just give her a dirty glare and say nothing. Will knew that his responses weren't helpful, yet he felt so correct in his opinions about good communication that he could hardly contain his reactions. He came to the conclusion that, if he was going to get along with his wife, he would need to make allowances for her imperfect style of communicating. This was very difficult for him to do, because it meant that he would sometimes have to set aside his feelings of being correct.

Setting aside correct notions in favor of becoming a harmonizer is one of the most unenviable tasks a marital partner could seek. Yet, we must remind ourselves that when two imperfect, sinful people join together in a marriage, they are not going to have total perfection. Therefore, since it is inevitable that flaws will occur in the relationship, it is helpful to be realistic in one's attitudes and beliefs.

Perhaps our attempts to hold correct beliefs in proper perspective will become easier if we remind ourselves what is subtly communicated when we become insistent.

Overt and Covert Communications

In virtually any communication, there can be two

kinds of messages emitted. In most defensive communications, both overt messages and covert messages are sent. Overt messages are the spoken words that are audibly received by the spouse. It is assumed that, when words are spoken, those words have a clear meaning that is understood by both partners. For example, a spouse who says "Leave me alone," presumably is communicating a message that he or she desires solitude. However, in the case of defensive communications, a covert message usually accompanies the overt. That is, there may be a hidden, unspoken meaning to the spoken words. For instance, the words, "Leave me alone," may really bear the message "I think you're a nuisance." The covert message is never audibly transmitted, but it is given and received nonetheless.

When a spouse uses an insistent means of speaking, there are usually several covert messages that accompany the overt words. Let's examine a few of them.

I Accept You with Conditions Attached

Whenever one spouse speaks insistently to the other, there is an underlying communication of conditional acceptance. It is as if the insistent spouse has a long unwritten agenda regarding how the partner should behave. If the partner successfully upholds the conditions set forth by the other mate, acceptance is given. But if the partner fails to live right, watch out! Acceptance is snatched away. The partner is usually put on probation until he or she amends his or her ways.

One of the easiest things to do is to accept others who are just the way we want them to be. Anyone can do that. The more difficult challenge is to offer acceptance to someone who is different or, particularly, to someone who is living wrongly. This forces us to set aside our personal ambitions and dogmatic thoughts in favor of the higher more taxing priority of love.

We see repeatedly in the writings about Jesus Christ

that he was able to hold firmly to his opinions regarding right and wrong while, at the same time, offer acceptance to those who lived counter to those beliefs. In fact, the majority of the times that his frustration was aroused occurred when peole held firmly to their rigid traditions without regarding others' need to be loved and accepted. We could state that a recurring theme in his ministry was one of love without conditions attached.

The insistent person's message of conditional acceptance can be so subtle that the sender may not even be aware it is being emitted. In innocence, this person may simply think that he or she is merely making a statement of opinion. So, in order to gain a heightened awareness of his or her own covert message, it would be helpful for the insistent partner to observe how such communication is received by the spouse. In most cases, the person on the receiving end of insistent messages will in some way express hurt, anger, or surprise. Rarely does insistent communication instill a positive, warm feeling in the recipient. This should be an obvious cue to the sender that while one's words may be based on right convictions, the message that is more penetrating is the one of non-acceptance.

I'm Superior to You

When insistent communication occurs, another covert message that is likely to be transmitted is one of superiority. For example, a wife may ask her husband to take a few minutes to talk with her regarding a disagreement they had about the children. The defensive husband responds by insisting that he doesn't have the time or desire to talk with her. In essence, he is communicating that he is above minor irritants and he shouldn't have to lower himself to talk about such matters. He subtly sends the message, "Who do you think you are, questioning *me*?"

An air of arrogance usually accompanies any kind of defensive, insistent mind-set. Whether the behavior takes on the form of a quiet withdrawal or a loud retort, the arrogance is painfully evident. By refusing to come down from one's opinionated position, this person is assuming that it would be improper to have to consider an inferior point of view.

Of course, it is obvious how this covert message of superiority can bring havoc to a marital relationship. No partner likes to be put into an inferior position by his or her mate. In fact, we all have a natural aversion to being talked down to. This is due to the fact that we each have an inborn desire to be treated with respect. This desire is evident in every human from the day of birth to the day of death. Therefore, communication implying a superiority can only add tension to a husband-wife relationship.

How does a defensive person develop this feeling of superiority? The ways of learning this pattern can be quite varied. Some people arrive at a feeling of superiority because they were protected in their early years from having to truly struggle with relationship issues. This can cause them to assume, idealistically, that they should never have to worry about having to go through the grind of hashing out differences in adult life. Others develop this superior attitude due to a high energy level that causes them to be very performance-minded. They are so keyed in to having to have successes that they scorn any thought of grappling with interpersonal weaknesses. Still others develop a superior attitude by growing up in an environment in which they frequently struggled in a position of inferiority. Wishing to escape such a position, they compensate by determining to avoid being placed in a lowly position again.

When one marital partner communicates to the other from a superior position, friction is guaranteed. This is due to the fact that the partner on the receiving end of the condescending message is automatically placed in the inferior position. And, since that partner will have an aversion to being in an inferior position, a counter-attempt may be made to gain superiority over the first mate. A never-ending "see-saw" effect can occur.

I Don't Trust You

When defensive partners hold insistently to their convictions, another covert message frequently transmitted is one of a lack of trust. The partner who offers resistance to the communication process is sending the message, "I'm hesitant to share my thoughts and feelings with you because I'm skeptical about your intentions." Perhaps the defensive partner can actually recall past instances when feelings were shared only to be stomped on by the mate. Yet, it is important for the insistent, defensive partner to recognize that a message of non-trust to one's partner can actually turn into a self-fulfilling prophecy.

I'm reminded of a wife who openly stated that she was afraid to share her feelings with her husband because she didn't trust his anger. The husband responded by saying that he became angry with her because she wasn't willing to trust him with her feelings. This wife failed to recognize that her lack of trust was indeed a factor in the very thing she didn't like in her mate.

In marital communications, we tend to set up the spouse's style of responding by the way we speak. For example, a partner who speaks calmly yet firmly is assuming that the spouse has an ability to appropriately comprehend the words spoken. A covert message of cooperation is extended in such an instance and communication has a strong chance of flowing smoothly. However, a spouse who is snappy or rude in speaking with his or her mate is merely asking for problems. Since the covert message is unflattering, so likely will be the partner's response to it.

Trust is one of the most crucial characteristics of a harmonious marriage. It is the bridge in communication that makes possible an open, honest exchange of feelings. And, contrary to common practice, trust is not a trait that must first be earned. Rather, it can be given. The spouse who gives trust instantly becomes more appealing. Usually, that spouse's mate then has extra motivation to give trust in return. A positive exchange can result.

Let's keep in mind that there are certain instances (such as in cases involving abuse or an affair) in which a partner will naturally be hesitant to offer complete trust. In such cases, a certain amount of defensiveness is predictable from both parties. Yet even then, when the spouses resolve to continue in the marriage, pursuing harmony, trust can be injected. Granted, it won't come overnight. Yet offering trust, even after a large disappointment, can be a key factor in the healing process. Withholding trust indefinitely only affirms one's insistent mind-set, which eventually can lead to a never-ending rut of defensiveness, and that's misery.

You Should Fit My Mold for You

An additional covert message that accompanies insistent communication is that of a defensive spouse insinuating that the partner should fit a prescribed mold exactly as it is spelled out in the defensive spouse's mind. These thoughts tend to run through the defensive partner's mind:

"My husband is wrong. Why can't he just act like he's supposed to (meaning like *I* want him to)?"

"If my wife would just do what I say, we wouldn't have any problems!"

"You're just going to have to be more patient and considerate. That's all there is to it."

"I'm not going to put up with someone who is always late. You'd better get your act together."

When defensiveness occurs, it points to the fact that the individual already has preconceived ideas about how the mate should behave. There is usually an accompanying assumption that if that mate would simply play out his or her role correctly (translation: my way), everything would work out just fine. Of course, this attitude is certain to prolong strife since it makes the spouse feel trapped.

No matter how right one's ideas are about what a good spouse should be, a major hitch occurs when one becomes insistent with these correct ideas, that is: *The partner's free will is denied.* Even though sinful mankind has abused the freedoms given to us by God, we are still offered free will. It is part of our inborn heritage. Galatians 5:1 states, "It was for freedom that Christ set us free; therefore keep standing firm and do not be subject again to a yoke of slavery." Presumably, this concept can be applied to the marriage relationship.

Don't get me wrong. I'm not advocating an "anything goes" philosophy of marriage. The Bible has plenty to say about the need for responsibilities in all relationships. The key point here is that no marriage partner has the right to dictate to the other how he or she must act. When this occurs, tension erupts and the possibility for rebellion is heightened.

By trying to make one's partner fit into a pre-planned mold, the defensive person is likely to experience the frustrations he or she so desperately abhors. This happens because the partner eventually feels imprisoned. A feeling of futility grows in the marriage and the partners begin to play games of "hide and seek" and "hit and run." As an illustration, one young husband shared with me that he didn't understand why his wife resented him so strongly whenever he offered her suggestions. We looked at some of his so-called suggestions and concluded that they would be more aptly labeled as commandments. With this in mind, we deduced that the wife felt she was supposed to fit his exact image of what she should be, which led to her disgruntled feeling of entrapment. No wonder he was having communication problems! He was living with a woman who felt tied down and incapable of living life as *she* determined proper.

This all points to the delicate fact that there needs to be a balance in the way we hold our beliefs in marriage. While it is beneficial for a spouse to have opinions and preferences, it is detrimental when they are then transformed into commands. The defensive mate who insists on getting his or her own way in marriage is perilously close to elevating self to an undeserved god-like position over the other.

Cater to Me

As a final thought, we can see that the insistent person is one who emits the covert message of wishing to be served. This person's mind-set assumes that certain rights and privileges belong to self as a result of being in the marriage.

As an example, perhaps a husband is resisting his wife's conversation regarding a visit that needs to be made with the in-laws. In his stubbornness, he sends the message: "But what about me! You know that's not what I want to do." Or maybe a wife has become edgy, because she perceives that her husband is not tuned in to her problems of taking care of the children. Angrily she covertly says: "You're so selfish that you never think about me. I demand that you notice my needs!"

The person who becomes insistent in marriage might justify this communication style by stating that it isn't wrong to take a stand for oneself, since self-preservation is a natural part of being human. And, technically speaking, that would be correct. Taking a stand for one's needs has its merits. And, we might add, there are times when the only way to grab someone else's attention is to speak firmly.

But what about the person who is *consistently* insistent or who demands his or her rights in an entirely unbecoming manner? Here we find an individual who has a problem with self-centeredness. This person seems to be living with the assumption that the world owes him or her a favor. There is a hint of grandiose feelings present. Usually, we find at the base of it all that this individual tends to be far more concerned about self's needs than the needs of the spouse. It is interesting to note that the Bible says little about demanding one's rights, while it has much to say about setting self aside (even when I am in the right). This is summarized in 1 Corinthians 10:24, which states, "Let no one seek his own good, but that of his neighbor." A consistent teaching in the scriptures is one of having self's needs met by becoming a giver. In marriage, this would mean giving away one's time, one's understanding, one's patience, or one's openness. There is less focus on what one will receive and more focus on the contributions being given.

Does this mean that an insistent spouse give up self defensiveness and become a martyr? No, not at all. Any person who lives with another person is eventually going to find the need to ask that the partner notice him or her. So the object of our attention is the partner's overall pattern. Although there are occasions to remind the spouse of personal wants and needs, when a partner lives in an overall pattern of insistence, it is an indication that there is a problem with too much self-focus.

Summary

There is a strong difference between stating one's opinions and demanding that one's spouse live in a specified manner. In this chapter, we have noted that there is much more to the communication practice than a mere expression of words. The underlying covert messages may actually be the more significant. Consequently, it is important, as spouses examine their styles of communication, that they take a long and hard look at these nonverbal signals. Hopefully, efforts will then be made to keep one's *entire* communication style consistent with the overall goal of harmony.

8

Anger:
The Troublesome Emotion

A further factor that contributes to a defensive nature is anger or, more specifically, the misuse and misunderstanding of anger. Ask any couple who has experienced resistant communication if they have had problems with the use of anger and you will get an affirmative answer every time! Anger is one of the least understood and most abused emotions there is. And it is always found in the thick of defensive communications.

Defensive partners tend to have one of two problems with anger. Either (1) they assume that virtually all anger is wrong and should be avoided as often as possible, or (2) they suffer from a lack of training and/or experience regarding the proper handling of anger. In either case, couples can become bogged down in their interactions because of their approach to this emotion. Let's examine these two problems separately.

Is All Anger Wrong?

Most people have grown up with the idea that anger is

an emotion that invariably will create strife. As children we each saw adults handle it in less than desirable ways, perhaps resorting to yelling or holding grudges. Likewise, we all grew up watching peers or siblings who would display anger inappropriately by being disobedient or rebellious. And those of us who grew up in the TV era saw that misguided anger often resulted in violence and even killings. Furthermore, we have all read newspaper accounts about anger in the streets in the form of robbery and murders. If we could count the number of times in our lives when we have witnessed the negative effects of anger, that number would reach literally into the thousands! No doubt, anger can be a violent, much maligned emotion. Therefore, it is easy to dismiss all anger as bad.

But if all anger was wrong, we would not have Ephesians 4:26 in the Bible tell us to "be angry, and yet do not sin." Nor would we be told in James 1:19 to "be slow to anger." (If all anger was bad we wouldn't be permitted even to be slow with it). Likewise, if all anger was wrong, we would then be forced to condemn the acts of Jesus Christ, who himself became angry to the point that he cleared out the temple in Jerusalem (Mark 11:15-17) and rebuked the hypocrisy of uncaring people (for one illustration, see Mark 3:1-5). Apparently, there can be times when anger can be a proper emotion. The Bible actually teaches us to have a very cautious, selective use of anger.

However, to keep anger in balance, we must remind ourselves that while there is a go-ahead given for anger in the Bible, it is a very conservative one. In fact, there are many direct teachings regarding the abuse of this emotion. For instance, Ephesians 4:31 tells us to put way anger that is accompanied by other such traits as bitterness, wrath, clamor, slander and malice. Proverbs 29:22 indicates that there is no benefit for a man who is hot-tempered. And Galatians 5:20 lists both strife and outbursts of anger as being "deeds of the flesh." So we see

112

that while there are indicators in the Bible that make allowance for anger, there are also warnings that encourage us to be very certain the anger does not get carried to destructive proportions.

When we examine the rights and wrongs of anger, it is safe to conclude that, since anger is an easily abused emotion, it should be used sparingly and judiciously. It definitely should not be the dominant emotion in a marriage. But we need not assume that anger should be eliminated altogether. Marital partners who hold a highly threatened or resistant attitude toward this emotion can actually create some of the friction they are so desperate to avoid. Let's look at what can happen in a marriage in which one of the partners allows for no anger.

Case Example

Janice and Alex had waited until their early thirties to get married. Neither had been in any hurry to get to the altar and both had been willing to wait until the right person came along before making this lifelong commitment. Because they were both patient in making the decision to marry, they assumed that they would have a much better than average relationship. And indeed, they did.

But even though Janice and Alex had a strong marriage, they had one major problem that caused them great concern. It was the problem of anger. To be sure, they weren't violent or abusive with their anger, yet it was felt more often than they had assumed it would be. Alex was the kind of person who became stern and harsh whenever his irritation arose, while Janice was prone toward manipulative silence in her anger. To say the least, an air of defensiveness permeated their home whenever this emotion arose. They were both concerned enough about this to come to my office to discuss the matter.

One of the first questions I asked them after they explained their problem was: "Is anger bad?" Both pairs of eyes opened wide as they nodded in unison. Alex explained: "I never wanted to have anger in my marriage, because it was such an awful emotion in my home as I was growing up." Janice had a completely opposite thought: "Well, my childhood was almost perfect. I just don't remember ever having to deal with anger in my home and I don't want to have to start now." As they each explained their thoughts further it became clear to me why they would become defensive at the onset of one another's anger. At that point we launched into a discussion that helped them understand anger and to realize that its presence didn't spell doom for their marriage.

In order to pursue harmony in marriage, we must first assume that anger is a natural emotion given to us by God for a specific purpose. It is paradoxical that, if we try to force anger out of a relationship, it only tends to build. But if we make room for it by understanding it and handling it properly, it tends to be less of a problem.

The Function and Uses of Anger

What is the proper function of anger? In order to answer this question, let's remind ourselves why people become angry in the first place. Think about the times when your anger is present and when it is not. You *don't* become angry when others are friendly, cooperative, understanding, and patient. But you *do* become angry (frustrated, annoyed, irritated) when you feel insulted, ignored, misunderstood, or unappreciated. In a majority of cases, anger comes about in the face of negative interactions. So what does this tell us about this emotion? Anger is tied in to a person's self-preservation system. Anger is the emotion that attempts to communicate: "Hey, notice my needs! I'm a somebody and I deserve to be treated fairly!" Anger is the emotion of self-advocacy.

Seeing anger in this light makes us acknowledge that it can have a positive function. After all, it is useful to an individual when taking a stand for self when self's needs or self-worth are being violated. Likewise, anger is a positive function to use when taking a stand for one's personal convictions and beliefs. Used carefully, anger can lead to a sense of respect and fair play in interpersonal relating.

The problem with anger, though, that leads to defensiveness is that it is most often *displayed* in ways that

114

undermine good communications. Even when the emotional individual feels angry for a legitimate reason, there still may be one of three major problems at work: (1) the *intensity* of anger doesn't match the magnitude of the problem, (2) there is such a *preoccupation* with self's needs that no effort is made to understand others' points of view, or (3) the anger is being expressed in an insensitive, inconsiderate manner. In any case, when anger is displayed without proper forethought and planning, it can turn completely sour, bringing nothing but dissatisfaction to a relationship. The fact that anger is handled in these manners so often explains why it has obtained such a nasty reputation.

Notice how a positive use of anger can easily turn sour and bring turmoil to a marriage.

Case Example

Wally had a bad habit of being snappy and irritable whenever his wife would ask him to help with various chores. For example, whenever she suggested that she needed a hand in the kitchen, he could usually be counted upon to flare up and say something about needing to have a few minutes to relax. It's not that he was necessarily wrong in asking that his wife consider his needs. But Wally's problem was that the frequency and intensity of his anger far exceeded what was necessary to voice his needs. Wally was so absorbed with his own desire for self-preservation that he was consistently defensive and insensitive to the needs and feelings of his wife. Usually, when his anger would come out in this edgy manner, his wife would feel hurt and would then feel prompted to give a comeback. Of course, this only caused Wally's irritation level to rise, and he and his wife would be well on their way to another evening of unhappiness with each other.

It is apparent that while anger can be positive in its original function (standing up for one's needs) the greatest problem with this emotion lies in knowing when and how to handle it. In order to come to the point of keeping anger under control, it would first be to our advantage to distinguish between the two kinds of anger, aggressive and assertive.

Aggressive Anger

Aggressive anger is defined as the act of taking a stand for one's needs, worth, or convictions in a manner that proves to be inconsiderate or insensitive to the needs of the one toward whom the anger is directed. This is the mode of anger used most often by defensive spouses, since it is normal for them to be less concerned with the welfare of others than with self. In addition, it tends to lead to a feeling of futility in marriage, because anger expressed aggressively rarely, if ever, helps bring constructive solutions to problems. In a harmonious marriage, this style of anger must be minimized as much as is humanly possible.

Aggressive anger may be quite obvious, but it can also be very subtle and sneaky. Let's look at some of the various kinds of behaviors that are a part of aggressiveness.

Open, hostile aggression. When we think of aggression, we tend to think of loud acts of hostility and rage. And, if we consider the definition of aggressive anger as being self-preserving yet inconsiderate, we can see that indeed this kind of behavior fits the description. Some spouses feel so overwhelmed with their need to take a stand for themselves that they readily resort to an extreme style of venting their feelings. This may be done by shouting or speaking in loud insulting tones. It may include a dramatic flailing of the arms and prancing around the room. Or it may take the form of acts of physical violence, such as hitting, throwing objects, or kicking furniture. Once spouses get into this mode of expressing anger, they tend to go on and on with little impulse control. Things are said that may later be regretted deeply. Behavior shown may be highly out of one's normal character. Needless to say, this open, hostile aggression never succeeds in accomplishing an atmosphere of harmony. It is to be avoided at all costs.

In a marriage characterized by defensiveness, it is not hard to imagine how this style of aggression can take place. When there is an air of frustration and tension, and when the communication easily bogs down in resistance, it is predictable that one or both partners will have anger building on the inside that eventually erupts in an explosive manner. When this occurs, it is not just the explosive spouse who needs to take a personal inventory of his or her communication style. The remaining spouse could also benefit by examining his or her communication style to see if there is some unintentional contribution made to such hostility.

Open, cutting behavior. Some spouses may not go to the extreme of uncontrollable hostility when their anger arises. They are a bit more tame in their expression of the emotion. Yet, there still is an aggressiveness in their communication because an inconsiderate mind-set is in action. Spouses who utilize the open, cutting style of aggression are prone to behaviors such as: being regularly critical, offering put-downs to a spouse who has goofed, using sarcasm to express frustration, complaining and whining about things gone wrong, being stubborn and inflexible in opinions, and putting blame onto the spouse when something isn't right. True to the nature of aggressive anger, this style of expression does little to bring harmony to the marriage. It only increases the already present frustration.

When defensiveness is a regular factor in marriage, this open and cutting style of aggression is almost always present. In attempting to protect oneself, the defensive partner may feel compelled to express frustrations by putting the partner in his or her place. More attention is paid to one's own needs than to the need for considerate assertions.

117

Passive-aggressive anger. There are some people who pride themselves in the fact that they rarely become aggressive (or so they think). They assume that because they don't yell or snap at their spouse, they are keeping their anger under control. But while their anger may not be expressed in loud or cutting ways, it often becomes apparent that these people merely express their aggressions in more passive, subtle ways.

Keep in mind that the definition of aggressive anger calls for one to take a self-preserving stand without being considerate of others involved. There are many underhanded ways in which this can be done. For example, aggressiveness can be passively expressed by giving a cold, silent stare. Words may not be shouted, but the distasteful message is still there. Other illustrations of passive-aggressive anger are laziness, procrastination, leaving the room, muttering beneath one's breath, staying away, and tuning out.

Passive-aggressive anger is almost always present in a defensive marriage. Since this style of anger is very evasive, it has an appealing lure to a marital partner who is seeking a safe means of self-protection with the least amount of personal accountability. Often, it can be the most difficult style of aggressiveness to break, because the passive-aggressive person tends to deny the extent of the anger that hides behind these passive behaviors. In order to avoid such behavior, the passive-aggressive spouse must first have a sense of honesty regarding the anger buried within.

Assertive Anger

For each inappropriate, aggressive means of expressing one's anger there is a corresponding positive way of expressing oneself. When a marital partner is working to control anger, it doesn't mean that this emotion has to be dismissed altogether. (That could lead to repression of one's basic needs, which would eventually fuel even greater levels of aggression.) Rather than being aggressive, a mate can choose to handle anger assertively.

Assertive anger is defined as taking a stand for one's needs, worth, or convictions while, at the same time, having a consideration and sensitivity for others' feelings. It differs from aggressive anger in that it involves a sense of humbleness and fair play on the part of the angry person. And because the assertive partner is seeking constructive solutions to problem situations, there is a strong possibility that the anger will be completed (done away with completely). If it is handled properly, anger won't keep coming back.

It is important to note that, when anger is used sparingly and assertively, the level of defensiveness in the marriage will decrease significantly. With this in mind, let's look at several ways that anger can be assertively expressed. As we examine the behaviors involved in assertiveness, keep one thought in mind: As a person is behaving assertively, he or she may not *look* angry (as we tend to envision anger). Rather, an assertive person is *nipping* the anger at a point before it builds into an ugly, destructive behavior.

Of course, one who has been used to perfect relationships, without a negative reaction to any behavior, may be able to practice all the following actions freely with no hesitancy or need for assertive anger. Few of us, however, live within such a perfect relational environment that we can attempt to take care of all these needs without expecting negative reactions, whether verbal or non-verbal, from time to time.

Following is a list of some common expressions of assertiveness:

1. Stating opinions and preferences tactfully.
2. Saying no when someone asks you to do something that will wreak havoc in your schedule.

3. Having a sense of family priorities and faithfully sticking to it.
4. Asking your spouse to help you in your chores.
5. Taking the time and effort to do an occasional favor for yourself.
6. Asking questions when you are confused.
7. Setting stipulations regarding your personal boundaries.
8. Calling for a brief truce when emotions begin to get carried away.
9. Taking a break in your schedule when you feel overloaded.
10. Being firm yet gentle in the way you express your feelings and needs.

Looking back over this list of examples of assertiveness, try to imagine what would happen emotionally to a person who fails to act in this manner at the necessary time. For example, a wife who feels the need to share her feelings of uncertainty about tentative plans for the weekend may not share those feelings with her husband, because she suspects he may disagree with her. What will be the likely result? Aggressive anger will build at a later point in time. By failing to act assertively at the proper moment, she is setting herself up for expressions of aggressiveness as the feeling festers and grows inside. By being calmly assertive at the right time, we can avoid later bouts with aggressiveness.

By examining the various choices of assertive and aggressive expressions of anger, it should be clear that we can have a good measure of control over anger. As we place our options on the table, we will determine that assertive expressions of anger will be far more successful than any of the aggressive behaviors. Couples who are entrenched in defensive communications (and consequently in insensitive anger) have usually not taken the time and energy to explore these options. Or, if they have, they quickly abandon their efforts if the spouse does not respond properly right away.

Knowing When to Drop Anger

A couple whose communication is characterized by defensiveness can greatly benefit by understanding the rights and wrongs of anger and the proper and improper expressions of it. But in any marriage there will come times when it still isn't enough for the couple to distinguish between correct and incorrect anger. By this I mean that there are times in the marriage when *no* anger is the best course to take. This usually comes when both spouses have valid points of assertion while still being at odds with each other.

Case Example

Randy was a hard-working executive who put all his energies into his job during his office hours. He was a go-getter who was proud of the fact that he was on his way to the top. He was known as the kind of worker who would take charge when something needed doing. But at home, Randy preferred to slip into a different mode of action. He was by no means lazy, but he couldn't be described as hard-driven either. His feeling was that home was his oasis and he didn't want to be pushed into a grinding routine there. His wife, Brenda, on the other hand, felt worn to a frazzle every evening when Randy would come home. Keeping track of three active kids was no piece of cake! Naturally, she looked forward to her husband's return home each night so that she could have a little relief.

You can imagine the potential this gave for resistant anger. When Brenda sought his help in the evenings on routine matters, Randy sometimes balked. His instinctive desire was to have some space. Brenda would feel hurt that he wasn't cooperating in the way she wanted and an argument would start. Both spouses would have legitimate points to make, but neither seemed willing to back down from their position until the other did so first. An irritating stand-off would be the result.

In cases in which both spouses have reasons to be assertive, and they honestly try to handle their anger sanely, there can still be a defensive outcome. So what's a couple to do when they get to this point?

When assertive anger fails to bring a constructive conclusion to the problem, a mate is faced with three possible choices: (1) to bury the anger and pretend it's not there when, in fact, it is, (2) to use one of the aggressive expressions of anger (as previously outlined) in an attempt to get one's way, or (3) to drop the anger and go on. In a defensive relationship, spouses tend to choose (1) or (2), but rarely do they make the third choice.

When individuals choose to drop anger, it means that they clearly recognize that they have come to a point where the anger no longer serves any useful function. They recognize that they may have a justifiable reason to take a stand for their needs and convictions but, if they continue to do so, the problems will only worsen. Therefore they make a conscious decision to dismiss the anger, deliberately choosing to set it aside. (Note: This is different from the repression of anger, since repression involves the act of kidding oneself into thinking the anger is gone when, in fact, it is clearly still in evidence.) It is at the point of dropping anger that a person exercises the utmost mental control over his emotions. This assumes that, with God's aid, we don't have to be consumed with our anger every time it surfaces.

Why do defensive people have a hard time letting go of their anger? Let's examine three major factors beneath an inappropriate angry mood.

Placing Right Beliefs over Profit

When a defensive mate holds too tightly to anger it is an indication that that person is clinging so firmly to what is right that a sense of what is profitable (beneficial) is lost. As mentioned in the last chapter, a defensive person can be very right in his or her beliefs while very wrong in the practice of communicating. Holding firmly to one's angry assertions, a spouse can quickly lose sight of the factors involved in creating an atmosphere of harmony.

I'm reminded of a wife who exclaimed, "How can I feel good about dropping my anger when my husband is acting inappropriately and I *know* I'm right?" My response was that she didn't necessarily have to feel good about dropping her anger. It can be much like the unhappy feeling a sports fan has after leaving a game in which the home team lost. He definitely is not pleased with the outcome, but he recognizes (hopefully) that continual griping and grumbling about the loss won't do any good either.

Often, a defensive person fails to recognize that a sense of love and harmony takes priority over what is right. This is why he or she may be prone to hold on to anger beyond the point of positive results. If this occurs frequently, it is an indication that this person needs to take a closer look at the inner goals and priorities that are directing the communications.

Having an Insensitivity to the Spouse's Feelings

Too often when a spouse refuses to drop anger, it is a sure signal of a lack of sensitivity to the mate's feelings and point of view. There is such a keen focus on self's needs that an inward tunnel vision occurs. This was illustrated to me when I questioned a young husband about the possibility of dismissing his anger rather than pushing it to the point of bringing turmoil to his marriage. He responded by saying, "Look, when I get mad I'm really not all that concerned with *what* it does to my wife's feelings. She is just going to have to accept the fact that things are going to have to change at our house!" It was clear that he was a prisoner to his own angry feelings, because he lacked sensitivity to his wife's needs, which would give him the objectivity he needed to gain control over his emotional tirades.

Second Timothy 2:24–25 tells us: "And the Lord's bond-servant must not be quarrelsome, but be kind to all, able to teach, patient when wronged, with gentleness correcting those who are in opposition." In this teaching is an implied assumption that we have the ability to take a stand for our convictions while, at the same time, have a balanced sense of fair play in our attitudes. The trait that will enable a spouse to have this sense of balance is sensitivity. Without it, a quarrelsome attitude is likely.

Personal Insecurities

An individual who has an inability to drop anger, once it is obvious that the anger is harmful, is a person who suffers from serious feelings of insecurity. Keep in mind that the function of anger is to take a stand for one's needs or worth. While we can say that it is a positive sign when a person has the desire to be an advocate for one's basic worth, it can become a negative trait when that person feels the need to stand up for self to the extent that he or she doesn't seem to know when to stop.

Think of this analogy. A sign of a healthy self-image is shown when a person is able to accept compliments and to feel comfortable about his or her personality and achievements. But what is your reaction to the individual who seems to be openly begging for compliments and who constantly wants others to focus on his or her wonderful personality traits and glorious achievements? If you're like me, you are probably skeptical of that person's feeling of security, wondering why there is such a need for constant ego boosts.

In a sense, the person who refuses to drop anger is like the individual who fishes for compliments or who boasts about his fine accomplishments. In both instances, the fact that this person takes too strong a stand for self is a sure signal that a feeling of neediness and uncertainty about self rests within. This points to the fact that, if a person is going to master the skill of knowing how to drop anger, there first must be an inner reconciliation of one's personal feelings of security and stability.

Summary

It is clear that a person who is attempting to set aside defensiveness in favor of pursuing harmony in marriage will be confronted eventually with the emotion of anger. In this chapter, we have assumed that it is actually possible to have a thorough understanding of anger's function and its expressions to the extent that we can exercise mental control over it. That is, the mind can act as a control base that oversees this emotion and how it either helps or hinders marital communications. The key to controlling anger rests in: (1) understanding biblical teachings on the subject, (2) being aware of the purpose or function of the emotion, (3) recognizing the various ways, positive and negative, that anger can be expressed, and (4) having the ability to discern when anger should be dropped.

9

Marital Myths

Another reason for the occurrence of defensiveness is found in the tendency of marital partners to hold on to unrealistic beliefs regarding what should or should not be expected in the marriage. In a sense, such couples have a mythological approach to matrimony. They assume that they know exactly how a marriage is supposed to unfold over the years. By clinging to such myths, these couples actually set themselves up for problems in their communications. (A myth is defined as a popular belief that is founded on a false notion.)

I'm reminded of one young bride who nearly had a nervous breakdown just a few weeks into her marriage because her new husband simply didn't perceive the world from her "woman's perspective." In anguish she would cry out, "What's wrong with him? Why can't he be more sensitive to me?" It was clear to her friends that she was living with the myth that her husband should just naturally have an intuitive feel for her innermost thoughts and attitudes. By holding to this myth, she was asking for heartache to camp at her door, and she was creating within herself a chronic problem with defensive marital communications. This woman is representative of many spouses who have brought undue stress upon themselves because they have clung to unrealistic fantasies.

When a couple holds onto marital myths, they are usually guilty of clinging only to romanticized notions without acknowledging the very real presence of imperfections in each other. Ideals are clasped without a full consideration of reality. Most myths have a measure of common sense to them, and they usually seem attractive on the surface. However, when all is said and done, marital myths tend not to make allowance for the humanity of the husband and wife. An underpinning of perfectionism is evident in them.

In order to continue our efforts to understand why defensiveness occurs, let's examine some of the common myths of marriage. Most couples who find themselves struggling with defensiveness usually are prone to using myths. By examining their beliefs, partners can eventually come to a realistic level of expectation regarding what can be expected in marriage.

Myth 1
A harmonious marriage is one in which there are no problems.

Wouldn't it be nice to live in a home where problems were nonexistent? Just imagine how it would be to get up each morning knowing that a cross word will never be spoken and, whenever communication occurs, there would be perfect understanding. That would be grand!

It's fun to allow our minds to wander into fantasyland for a few moments. But when we begin thinking about the possibility of a marriage with no problems, we must pinch ourselves to get back to reality. There has been only one couple in the history of mankind that knew perfect marital bliss. That couple was Adam and Eve. Before their willful decision to try to out-think God, they really had it good. Adam was never late for meals. He never had to be reminded of his manners. He never argued or talked back. He was the epitome of a perfect gentleman. Likewise, Eve was always a perfect supporter for her husband. She always knew the right things to say to him. And she always looked spiffy! But that was before sin.

Once sin entered their lives and, consequently, the lives of all their descendants, defensiveness became a common trait for them. They had arguments. They had lapses in their sexual relations. They lacked full understanding of each other's moods. With the onset of sin came a whole host of marital tensions that were relayed from their generation to the next.

As long as mankind has sin to grapple with, there will be problems in marriage. Some couples have greater control over problems than others. Nonetheless, no marriage is excluded. The successful couples, therefore, will be the ones who make allowance for the fact of sin to the extent that they aren't unduly upset by the disagreements that are guaranteed to be present.

Myth 2
Everyone (particularly Christians) should know what a good husband or wife is.

There are two kinds of knowledge, head knowledge and experiential knowledge. If asked to give a description of a proper husband-wife combination, most couples could do pretty well in explaining how patience, sensitivity, and trust should be a part of that relationship. In other words, most of us have an adequate amount of head knowledge. But when it comes to experiential knowledge, it is an altogether different story.

Think on this question. How many of us can remember times during our formative years when we had long chats with parents, ministers, or teachers about the skills and attitudes needed to implement the head knowledge given to us? Too few, I'm afraid. The fact is that many adults are woefully inexperienced in the ability to take head knowledge and translate it into deep-seated attitudes that profoundly affect their marital behavior. They may know that they're supposed to be sensitive, for example, but when it comes to knowing how to put sensitivity into experience, there may be a large gap.

This all points to the fact that a person may be able to cite good information about successful marriage without having the experiential background of knowing how to fully integrate those truths into his or her way of life. Therefore, we can never just assume that a mate should somehow know how to be a good marital partner. In many instances, training is badly needed.

Myth 3
A good marriage should just happen without strenuous amounts of work.

Many times I've heard couples complain that they felt cheated because their marriage took so much effort to maintain. Assuming that good marriages should just come together, they feel frustrated when they are required to put in hours of overtime in making things click. Naturally, couples who believe that good marriages should "just happen" will find themselves reacting defensively when the truth becomes evident that some extra "elbow grease" is needed in the relationship.

When couples live with the myth that a good marriage should just happen, they often cite the fact that they have had other friendships and family ties that were easily maintained. So why, they reason, does the marriage take so much more work? When people develop this manner of thinking, they are failing to acknowledge that no relationship comes close to having all the intricacies of a marriage. So many extra factors go into the making and maintaining of a good marriage that it is unfair to compare it to any other relationship.

For example, when spouses have disagreements, they aren't able to go their own separate ways without contact for a week (as we are able to do in our friendships). Rather, they have the same bed to sleep in, meaning that solving the problem has a sense of urgency. Being much closer, their problems can take on larger proportions, which means that more work is required. Because there is a greater amount of closeness in a marriage and because the intimacy level to be achieved is so different from any other relationship, it is only predictable that more effort will be required of husbands and wives.

Myth 4
If spouses love each other, the sexual aspect of marriage will take care of itself.

As a spinoff of Myth 3, some couples merely assume that pleasant sexual activity will just naturally occur if the couple can learn to communicate positively in their day-to-day routines. But when couples hold this myth, they may find they are easily disappointed in themselves if their sexual relationship seems stiff. These couples need to recognize that the sexual aspect of marriage takes as much (or sometimes more) work as the other aspects of communication. (Remember: sex is a form of communication.)

People who have studied sexuality agree that no two individuals can be expected to have the same level of sexual interest and proficiency. There are many biological and emotional factors that are a part of each person's sexual make-up. And, in fact, these various factors can be so complex (perhaps subconsciously so) that there are very few couples who can expect to have a perfect match in this area. Each spouse has differing levels of need re-

131

garding the desire to love and to be loved. Each has different ways of expressing intimacy. Each has different physiological drives. Therefore, it is quite natural to assume that, even if a husband and wife get along well in their mundane routines, extra amounts of effort may still be required in the area of sexuality.

Myth 5
Honesty is always the best policy.

At first glance, it would seem silly to state that couples shouldn't have full honesty with each other. After all, if a marriage was built on lies and deceit it would be very shaky. So deception definitely has no positive place in a relationship. Yet, it is a fact that some spouses sometimes use the "honesty is the best policy" philosophy to the detriment of their marriage. For example, one woman shared with me how she assumed that she always had to be honest with all her feelings in marriage. So she proceeded to share with her husband how she had harbored feelings of hate and resentment toward him in the past and how she feared that those feelings could easily return. Unfortunately, the husband was hurt by such honesty to the extent that his sense of trust in his wife diminished. But, jumping onto the honesty bandwagon, he shared his own negative feelings with her. As a result, their love for each other eventually soured to the extent that they decided, if they were having such feelings toward each other, they shouldn't have married. They had been honest with each other, but it had worked against them. They needed to recognize that there may be times when sensitive diplomacy takes higher priority to cold honesty.

Myth 6
Spouses should always enjoy the same activities

132

and should spend most of their free time with each other.

Some marriage partners put heavy pressure on themselves by assuming that their interests and activities should be intricately intertwined. They assume that if one spouse is highly social and the other is socially reserved, then it must mean that theirs is a bad marriage. (You can see where this would lead to defensive communication.) A feeling of failure can result when couples come to the conclusion that their personalities are just too different.

Actually, there is a lot of truth to the old adage that variety is the spice of life. Rather than being threatened by the fact that they are not together in all pursuits, partners can take pleasure in the fact that there is variableness in their lives. On a practical level, this means that a wife need not feel guilty if she doesn't share her husband's enthusiasm for sports activities. Or a husband need not feel poorly about his marriage if he can't get into his wife's chatter about the weekend party with the church group. When husbands and wives are able to enjoy activities away from each other, it can actually enrich the time they do spend together. It may be that they will need to structure special times in order to find a happy middle ground where they both can share common activities, but with a spirit of tolerance and cooperation, enjoyment of mutual activities is a very reachable goal.

Myth 7
When the romance is gone, the love left is no good.

One of the most pleasurable aspects of a male-female union is the sharing of romantic, sentimental moments. Most of us can recall the emotional highs we have felt whenever we had special candlelight dinners or moonlit strolls on the beach. Few experiences can top these.

But what about those times when the romance just isn't there? Does that mean the marriage is a lost cause? Not necessarily. While it is desirable for couples to be able to share romantic moments throughout life, it does not spell doom to the relationship when the romance is gone. After all, a love that is founded strictly on romance is bound to be shaky anyway. When the Bible speaks of having a love for each other (for example, in 1 Cor. 13 or Eph. 5) it emphasizes a love that is action-oriented, based on willful decisions. This means that when husbands and wives lose the feeling of sentimentality for each other, they can still continue in their efforts to inject love into their relationship by exercising the will to act in loving ways toward each other. As they persist with their attitude of choosing to love, the feelings will have a chance to grow to the desirable level.

Myth 8
When anger is felt, it means that the relationship is a sour one.

Perhaps the most threatening emotion to any relationship is anger. No mate enjoys having anger at the heart of the marriage. Anger is usually unpleasant and we all know that it can lead to disruptive behavior if we are not very careful with it. And yet, distasteful though it may be, anger does not represent the "kiss of death" to a marriage.

Let's reiterate one thought that has already been expressed: No marriage is perfect. All marriages will have their moments of tension as long as the spouses have sin in their lives. Now, this doesn't mean that all marriages are bound to have wild explosions of anger. Such anger should be avoided at all costs. But it does mean that we will know moments of frustration and annoyance.

When those times come, the *worst* reaction a spouse can have is to become highly threatened by the other's frustrations. By allowing the threat, the spouse is only inviting the anger to become more powerful and long-lasting. Rather, harmony can be maintained when marital partners allow for the fact that they and their spouse will occasionally feel annoyed. And, rather than being upset about it, tolerance and patience can be exercised toward the irritated one. This means that when anger is felt, spouses agree to sit down and talk through those feelings in a rational manner so the anger won't be blown out of proportion.

Myth 9
Marriage should be the ultimate cure for loneliness.

One of the major reasons that prompts individuals to get married is that marriage offers people a place of belonging. We all have an inward desire to belong to someone. We all enjoy the feeling of being interpersonally connected, knowing that there is at least one person in the world who knows and understands our innermost feelings. In fact, we can go back to the original marriage of Adam and Eve and note that it was God's desire that Adam should have a mate, because he did not want Adam to be alone (see Gen. 2:18). Marriage was designed by God to be a safeguard against feelings of loneliness.

It is ironic, then, that while the first marriage relationship was designed to decrease the possibility of loneliness, the first experience of loneliness occurred as a result of deceptiveness that took place in that very relationship. This means that we humans have allowed marriage to take on the very aspect of life—loneliness—that God meant for marriage to avoid. So, in all humbleness, as we each allow for the imperfection of our ways, we need to acknowledge that, in marriage, it is predictable that we will at times feel the emptiness that God desired we not feel. We are instructed to aim for perfection in all aspects of our lives (Matt. 5:48), yet we can realistically expect to experience some of the feelings of isolation that marriage was meant to deter. When we acknowledge that occasional moments of isolation may occur in marriage, the feeling of loneliness tends not to be so devastating.

Myth 10
When something goes wrong in the marriage, someone should be blamed.

One of the fundamental problems in a defensive marriage is the problem of blame. It seems as if, when problems occur there is almost a reflex reaction to quickly ascertain who is at fault. Most of us have been overtrained in the notion that when something goes wrong we should set out to find the guilty party. However, if we examined this tendency to determine how helpful it is in building solid marriages, we would admit that blame-finding does little to aid any relationship.

When problems occur, couples would be more successful if they asked the question, "What is *my* current responsibility in the matter?" Rather than focusing on who caused the problem, they can be more successful when their energies are spent in determining how they can contribute to a solution. In practical terms, this means that when marital communications become tense, the husband and wife would be most likely to resolve their difficulty when each seeks to do something immediately to ease tensions.

In looking over these ten myths of marriage, the key attitude to be pursued is one of realism over idealism. When marital partners cling to perfectionistic ideals they are only asking for increased problems. By dropping the myths, couples may be forced to let go of a few romantic dreams, but they will find that the resulting atmosphere will be less tense. Consequently, harmony will be more possible.

Case Example

Ron and Doris had been married for seventeen years. Seemingly they had the ideal marriage and family life. They rarely argued, they had model children, and they were well respected in their church and in the neighborhood. Anyone who saw them together would suppose that their relationship was one to be envied.

But one day Ron sat Doris down to explain to her that he had been having an affair for approximately a year. He told her that he had sought counsel from a minister who had told him that he should drop the affair and seek his wife's forgiveness. He had felt guilty for some time regarding this illicit relationship, so he explained to Doris that they would both need to work with each other to reestablish a true closeness in their lives. (It was apparent that, while they had gotten along well over the years, there had been a great superficiality to their relationship.)

As anyone would imagine, the news of the affair sent Doris into a tailspin. She cried for hours in anguish. She questioned herself regarding her fitness as a wife; she questioned Ron regarding the sincerity of his stated desire to make things work; she questioned God for allowing this to happen. Understandably, she had a hard time knowing how to handle her problem.

But as the initial shock began to wear off, Ron and Doris began to seriously evaluate their marriage, trying to figure out why things had turned sour after so many years. As they rehashed their past, one theme kept becoming apparent to them. They recognized that throughout their adult lives they had been very perfectionistic regarding what the marriage was *supposed* to be. They had married with a "happily ever after" assumption about their relationship. They had assumed that they should never argue or have problems. They had hoped that their home would be a perfect haven from the dog-eat-dog world that they each saw in the business sphere. In essence, they had lived with strong mythical ideas about how their relationship should be nothing less than a match made in heaven. Consequently, the strain had become too great for Ron and he had looked for a way out.

Recognizing the need to reestablish more realistic expectations for their marriage, they both decided to admit to each other, for the first time, that their marriage would not be perfect. Their household was never going to represent the perfection of the "Ozzie and Harriet" harmony they had both assumed they were supposed to have. They acknowledged to each other that, in order to have a truly successful marriage, they would have to work daily to make allowances for their individual weaknesses, even as they were striving to bring about improvements in their communications.

At first, it seemed strange to both Ron and Dorris to admit that they would actually have to work at their relationship. And yet, as they progressed in this manner, they found success because the burden of perfectionism had been lifted and they were finally being real with each other for the first time in seventeen years.

It is ironic that when spouses drop the myths and recognize the flawed nature of their relationship, the marriage is then most likely to grow strong. By making allowance for the fact of their own imperfections, spouses are relieved of the tremendous strain of trying to prove that they are beyond the problems of common sinners. Think of this analogy. No sports team enjoys losing. In fact, it is the desire of every team member to win each game. Yet, if athletes live with the illusion that they are failures because they lose a game, a negative momentum can begin whenever a loss occurs. But if the team realistically acknowledges the fact that losses are a part of the game, then when they lose they can think to themselves, "We'll get 'em next time."

In the same manner, when spouses find that they are unable to always win in every aspect of marriage, they can take it in stride by thinking, "We may not be perfect, but it doesn't mean that we have to give up on ourselves. We'll keep going, in spite of our flaws."

Part Three

The Pursuit of Harmony

10

The First Peter Principle

Ask a choirmaster to describe his or her objective as the director of a group of singers and you will quickly be told that he or she desires to train musicians to blend their voices in a manner that creates a pleasing, unified interpretation of the musical score. While the choir members have voices that are entirely different from one another in pitch and strength, the choirmaster will work to skillfully blend their intonations into a congruent, well pitched, balanced sound. In fact, diversity is preferred among the singers, because it gives the choirmaster a chance to have a deeper quality of music. Rather than trying to make each person sing the same as the person sitting next to him or her, the choirmaster will be most pleased to get each voice to complement the other. Harmony is preferred over monotony. The variances among voices actually work to the choirmaster's advantage.

So often I hear couples complain that they are unable to have successful marriages because their personalities are so different. Retreating into defensive mind-sets, they proclaim, "If only we could get rid of our differences!" But when I think of the skillful choirmaster who is able to turn differences into beautiful harmony, I am prompted to respond to these people by encouraging them to seek ways to become unified even with their variances.

A harmonious marriage is not one in which there is sameness (of thought, emotions, or desires). Rather, a harmonious marriage is one that blends the personality traits of the husband and wife into a synchronized unit. When the Bible gives instructions about living the life of patience and kindness, it never adds the phrase, "*if* you think you have enough similarities with that other person." In giving us the various teachings on human interactions, the Bible presumes that harmony can be pursued no matter what personality differences are involved.

One woman shared with me a discovery she made. "It finally dawned on me that my husband and I will always be different. But that doesn't mean we can't love each other. I don't have to try to change my personality or his before we can get along." With this insight, she was able to make a realignment in her communication style so that it was far more cooperative and productive than it ever had been. She was able to put her energies toward being a harmonizer rather than trying to create a sameness.

We can be assured that there is a way to develop a cooperation in marriage. God has given us some very helpful, specific guidelines that will lead us toward healthy, satisfying relationships if we will but follow them. Rather than living with the perpetual frustration of a defensive marriage, we can commit ourselves to knowing and applying the principles he has set forth.

In this chapter, we will focus specifically on a section of Scripture that explains how we can have satisfaction in our relationships. I call this the First Peter Principle.

Let all be harmonious, sympathetic, brotherly, kind-hearted, and humble in spirit, not returning evil for evil, or insult for insult, but giving a blessing instead; for you were called for the very purpose that you might inherit a blessing.

1 Peter 3:8-9

These words penned by the apostle Peter were written to Christians in need of guidance because they were living in a world that did not comprehend the Christian way of life. Because it would have been so easy to become sidetracked in their interpersonal pursuits, Peter outlined for them the formula for successful living.

Since this passage is so rich in its instruction, it would be to our benefit to break it down, thought by thought, in order to garner from it the fullness of its message. Although this passage has inferences for all Christians, we will focus on how it specifically relates to marriage partners. As we examine the specifics in this passage, we will notice that there are two distinct aspects of personal relations that are identified—inward traits and outward communications.

Inward Traits of Cooperation

In verse 8 of Peter's teaching, we find that he lists five *inner* characteristics that are crucial to thriving relationships: harmony, sympathy, a brotherly spirit, kindheartedness, and humility. As these inner traits are assimilated within the minds of husbands and wives, it would only follow that the traits of *outer* communications listed in verse 9 would then be attainable.

We will focus in on the characteristics identified by Peter that are so vital to marital success.

Spouses Are to Be Harmonious

It is no coincidence that the apostle places the trait of being harmonious at the beginning of his list. As we each seek to inject harmony into our relationships, it would be logical to assume that the other positive traits mentioned in the passage would be more easily attained.

The call for harmony by Peter is more of an appeal toward unity of disposition rather than unity of opinion. In this passage, he is suggesting that partners can have a like-mindedness in that they can agree to pursue such traits as patience and gentleness with equal fervor. Even if they disagree in areas such as politics or religion, partners can still respond to one another with loving words and actions. Unity can be attained due to a commitment to be Christ-like, regardless of apparent variances in character and thought.

I recall one woman who for years had regretted the fact that she and her husband were so opposite in personal preferences. Repeatedly, she had told herself that she would be able to get along with him *if only* he had likes and dislikes more similar to hers. But when she heard a speaker at a seminar explain how a Christian, guided by God's power, could be cooperative with virtually any kind of person, a light clicked on in her mind. "It's so refreshing to think that I can have harmony at home, even though my husband and I disagree!" She made a new commitment to her marriage, knowing it didn't have to be perfect to be rewarding.

It's easy to be harmonious with someone who is just like you. Anyone is capable of that. Jesus Christ, recognizing the tendency we all have to mingle only with our own kind, once asked the rhetorical question, "For if you love those who love you, what reward will you get?" (Matt. 5:46). He went on to teach the principle of living in love, even with those who are in direct opposition to us. As spouses seek to apply this notion to their marriage they will find themselves less preoccupied with the need to make changes in each other and more concerned with creating the atmosphere of unity so vital to a thriving marriage. While it is nice for partners to have a oneness in opinions, it is far more necessary that they have a oneness in spirit.

Spouses Are to Be Sympathetic

So often when we think of sympathetic behavior, we have the idea of a funeral-like demeanor. But as this word is used in 1 Peter 3:8, it has the connotation of sharing fellow feelings, whether they be joyful or sad.

In a thriving marriage, one of the most vital characteristics for growth is a willingness to openly enter into and share the feelings of one's spouse. In this situation, spouses are willing to rejoice with each other in happy moments and cry with each other in low times. More than just sharing activities together, sympathetic spouses desire to bring a depth to their relationship by being keenly interested in the things that are closest to each other's hearts.

A major complaint in marriages characterized by defensive communications is that at least one partner is stubbornly hesitant to let the other know what he or she is feeling. More often than not, the closed spouse is the husband, although I have known wives who have suffered from the nonsharing mentality.

Case Example

Roy shared with me how he had lived his first fifty years with a crusty disposition. "I never did talk with my wife about feelings, hers or mine, because I didn't think they were very important." However, he and his wife had drifted so far apart in this kind of marriage that they almost came to the point of divorce. Roy's wife very clearly stated that she was tired of living with a man who cared nothing for her feelings and who seemed to have no soft side to his personality.

It was at this low point that Roy made a shift in his thoughts about personal relationships. He began thinking that maybe there was some truth to the idea that humans were placed together for reasons pertaining to emotional and spiritual togetherness. Once his wife finally caught his attention, he decided to make a real effort in getting to know

145

her deepest feelings and then sharing with her his innermost thoughts. In doing so, his marriage took on a depth never before experienced.

In order to avoid the frustrations of a closed marriage and to become truly sympathetic, spouses must have two major traits:

1. They must first be in touch with their own feelings. This means that they will understand how to identify such emotions as anger, guilt, depression, loneliness, and worry. And, once identified, they will have a willingness to openly declare these moods to their partner. By sharing one's own feelings openly, the partner is made to feel more relaxed and encouraged about sharing his or her feelings in return.
2. They must have an empathy for the spouses' feelings. *Empathy* is a word that implies that there is an understanding of the other person's emotions, as if one was in that other person's shoes. Spouses who use empathy are not nearly as concerned with telling a partner what he or she should do with their problems as they are in communicating a grasp of the partner's inner feelings. Empathy assumes, first, that one cares about the feelings of the other and, second, is willing to communicate that care.

Spouses Are to Be Brotherly

The third trait listed by the apostle Peter, in the passage we are focusing on, is that of brotherly love. Literally, he is alluding to the kind of camaraderie that exists between physical brothers and sisters. He is encouraging Christians to have a family-type love for one another and for those with whom they come in contact. In addition, a person who exhibits a brotherly nature is one who is friendly and companionlike, wishing good fortune on others.

One thing that invariably warms my heart is a husband-and-wife team enjoying the dimension of companionship. I'm encouraged when I witness marriage partners who are able to have a buddy relationship. They have a richness in their lives that makes them feel relaxed and content.

Many times I've heard the question, "Why can't husbands and wives be friends with each other?" (As you would suspect, those who ask this question are usually entrenched in a less than satisfactory relationship.) The answer to this question lies in the fact that spouses who find it hard to be brotherly are usually unwilling to view marriage as a relationship that requires constant attention to trivial details. There is a lack of focus on the notion that the most important human relationship one can have is marriage, meaning that it necessitates extra levels of attention in day-to-day matters. In fact, I often discover that spouses don't share a brotherly kind of love because one or both of them feel that this is an inferior trait to romantic love. They may take the attitude that if they can't have a high level of sentimentality in their marriage, they don't want to have to settle for what may seem to be a lower form of relating.

When we think in realistic terms, though, most of us will admit that a brotherly attitude toward one's spouse is actually a very practical attitude to maintain. After all, the majority of the time shared by husbands and wives is consumed in mundane routines of home life (eating together, going shopping, household chores). Therefore, when an attitude of companionship is actively pursued, these routine matters can take on the dimension of pleasure because they are being performed as one friend for another.

Spouses Are to Be Kindhearted

A further trait of a growing relationship is one in which a kindhearted nature is prominent. To be kindhearted means that warmth and tenderness permeates one's style of interaction. A feeling of affection is freely expressed, as is a sensitivity to the most personal needs of others. When Peter included this characteristic of kindheartedness toward others in his formula for relational success, he was expressing a thought similar to the one found in Ephesians 4:32, which states, "And be kind one to another, tenderhearted, forgiving each other, just as God in Christ also has forgiven you" (NASB).

Of all the individuals who have been successful in incorporating the trait of kindheartedness, we can find no greater example than Jesus Christ. A gentle, affectionate spirit was the hallmark of his personage. In fact, Jesus once summarized his desire for being kindhearted by telling his disciples, "Peace I leave with you; my peace I give you" (John 14:27). It was his goal to offer love in such a way that others would be infected with it. He has set the example for us to follow.

If we follow his example, we too will have a burning passion to present ourselves to our mates in a pleasant, agreeable fashion. We will seek to do the small things that are involved in communicating warmth. On a practical level this might mean that a husband will go out of his way to do an unexpected favor for his wife, merely for the sake of bringing her pleasure. And he will draw attention to the chores she regularly performs by praising her and giving her compliments. In addition, he will be ready with a gentle touch when he has casual conversations with her. He will have a consistent attitude of cooperation.

Likewise, the wife will be thrilled to do what she can to make her husband feel relaxed and at ease when he is in her presence. She will remind him that he is an important person that she respects. She will try to anticipate his likes and dislikes and will do what she can to communicate her willingness to serve.

When husbands and wives make a joint effort to incorporate an attitude of kindness in their everyday lives, they will find happiness. They may not always agree on opinion and philosophy, but they can have a oneness of spirit.

Let's remind ourselves that kindness is a choice. It takes concentration to successfully create such an atmosphere in the home. I'm reminded of a man who complained that he was not able to be kind to his wife because he had such a history of being ornery. But as we talked, we both concluded that his real problem was not in his ability to speak warmly or to act in a gentle manner. Rather, his problem was that he was not accustomed to having to think about what he was doing in his relationships. He had the problem that so many others have: he had the knowledge of what he could do, but he lacked the application. A kindhearted disposition, by definition, requires outward deeds of compassion.

Spouses Are to Be Humble in Spirit

The final inner trait in our formula for thriving relationships, humbleness, is a fitting conclusion for our discussion. Actually, the trait of humbleness is implied in each of the four previously discussed traits. It takes humility to be a harmonizer, as well as to be sympathetic, brotherly, and kind. To be humble is the opposite of being high-minded or haughty. It means that one does not have a tendency to brag or to impose oneself in any way onto another. A humble person is able to find joy in others' success. (We will spend more time discussing humility in Chapter 12.)

No one will be able to be successful in any sustained relationships if his or her needs are primary. The Christian philosophy of relationships is based on the principle of denying self in an attempt to offer gain to others. It is ironic but, when a person sets his or her needs aside, precisely at that time one's relationships with others have the best chances to succeed. As self-denial increases, the giving of oneself increases. And it is at that point that relationships reach new depths.

The Outward Results of a Harmonious Spirit

Just as 1 Peter 3:8 tells us of the inner qualities needed for successful relationships, 1 Peter 3:9 tells us what they will do for our communication practices. In verse 9, three communication traits are pointed out.

Not Returning Evil for Evil

The instruction to not return evil for evil involves both word and deed. We can remind ourselves that each individual is brought into this world with the natural tendency to sin. Therefore, the normal reaction for a sinful person is to strike out in an evil (sinful) way when faced with another's wrongdoing. But we are taught in the Scriptures that when a person becomes a Christian he or she becomes a new kind of creature, one who puts aside the old nature (see 2 Cor. 5:17). This means that spouses seeking to implement Christian principles in their marriage will be different. Instead of responding to harshness with harshness, there will be an effort to follow the teaching of Jesus: "This is my commandment, that you love one another" (John 15:17).

One couple who had successfully moved from a defensive, caustic marriage to one of true Christian harmony can tell many humorous stories about their past tendency of exchanging evil for evil. (At least now those stories are funny.) This couple tells how they would deliberately do things to pay back the other for wrongs committed. For example, the wife shared how she had been known to flavor meals with spices that she knew her husband didn't like when she felt slighted by him. Or she might promise to do him a favor and then deliberately forget to do it to secretly punish him for a "crime" he had committed. She recalls doing petty misdeeds (like taking his shirts to the cleaners and leaving them there until he had no more shirts to wear to work) in order to make him appreciate the chores she did.

Her husband admits now that he was no angel, either. When he felt mistreated by his wife it was not at all uncommon for him to go out drinking after work without calling her, leaving her to sit at home and fume. He had been known to take his wife's car keys away from her when they were having a circular argument, telling her that he would not let her have them until she agreed with his side of their argument. This couple had become so caught up in returning evil for evil that it had lowered them to the level of acting in childish, self-centered ways.

When I talk with couples who are caught in a spiral of vindictive behavior, as this couple had been, I encourage them to examine the traits listed in 1 Peter 3:8. I remind them that Christian marriages were designed for the purpose of *giving* love and building up the spouse. I encourage each of them to take the initiative to refrain from reacting to wrongdoing with a wrongdoing. It takes maturity of thought to do this, and it takes a vision of the overall purpose of marriage. It also makes just plain, common sense to become a harmonizer by refraining from the temptation to do evil.

When I encourage spouses to resist the temptation to return evil for evil, I also discuss with them the idea that one's behaviors do not have to hinge on what the other partner does. This means that if one spouse chooses to have an ugly spirit, the other is under no obligation to be ugly also. Rather, each spouse can personally determine to live for the Lord *regardless* of the other's actions. When this occurs, a sense of personal accountability to God is enacted in each partner and each is less likely to be a mere reactor to the other.

Not Returning Insult for Insult

It follows that if spouses agree to refrain from evil they will also refrain from exchanging insults. Partners who are pursuing harmony in marriage know that it is bad if one spouse feels the need to be insulting, and it is even worse when both speak in a derogatory manner. (Looking back to Chapter 3, you will find that partners who exchange insult for insult are susceptible to the boomerang style of defensiveness.) A partner who returns an insult when insulted is like a person who has dirty hands and chooses to wash them in a mud puddle. The condition only goes from bad to worse.

In Proverbs 15:1 we are told, "A gentle answer turns away wrath." So instead of being the kind of person who is willing to engage in verbal warfare, a Christian spouse will seek to invoke God's love. While this practice calls for a great amount of self-restraint, it is very attainable for the person who has the attitude of being a harmonizer. Individuals who are successful harmonizers rather than insulters are ones who have reminded themselves that they do not want to have a reputation of being spiteful and irritable. They have weighed the option of being vindictive against the option of being loving and have specifically and deliberately chosen to be loving. They recognize that, while they may have an instinct to offer cutting remarks, such behavior has no value or benefit.

Giving a Blessing Instead

Peter's principle for successful relationships follows a logical progression. He states that a person who chooses to refrain from evil and insults is one who understands the importance of offering a blessing and then acts on that. The person who is able to follow this teaching of being an upbeat, giving person is one who understands the meaning of living with others as unto God.

Case Example

Tony shared with me how he had lived his first thirty-four years as an irritable, defensive grouch. "Les, I understand clearly why I was so unhappy in my family life. I was constantly on edge, ready at any moment to hurl an insult toward my wife. And I didn't even blink at the thought of doing things that I knew would cause my wife grief. In all honesty, I can say that I was just a mean old crank!"

At age thirty-four, when he should have been coming into the peak of life, Tony was at the bottom. He had endured eleven years of an unhappy marriage (most of which was admittedly his fault). He had a cold and uncaring attitude toward his co-workers and neighbors. Although he was a member of a local church, his Christianity meant little to him. He wavered between moods of anger and depression. It was at this point that he sought counseling.

In his counseling, Tony readily began to have insights into his gruff demeanor. He began to understand how his poor self-image had been a factor in his distasteful mannerism, and he began to get a grip on his misuse of anger. And yet, as time went on, he still was not feeling victorious. There was some mysterious ingredient missing in Tony's way of life. A trained counselor would understand Tony well, so I said to him, "You're having a better understanding of who you are and why you behave the way you do. But tell me, how are you coming in openly communicating the love of God to your wife?" With this question, Tony knew the counselor had hit the nail on the head. He was increasing in his intellectual knowledge of himself, but he knew his life would not be complete until that knowledge was followed by right behavior.

I went on to sort through some of the specific options of loving behavior. We then spent the bulk of our time focusing on Tony's need to give a blessing to others with no hope or expectation of a reward in return. He was convicted of the fact that he needed to give of himself, simply for the sheer joy of giving. When he incorporated this behavior into his lifestyle, life became a joy.

In 1 Peter 3:8-9, the apostle gives us a formula for living which includes cultivating inner traits which affect our outlook on life and in turn influence our outward communications. He then closes this eloquent passage by reminding us, "For you were called for the very purpose that you might inherit a blessing."

First, we seek to have the fine inner attitudes of harmony, sympathy, brotherly love, kindheartedness, and humility. Then, we seek to implement those inner attitudes by refraining from evil and insults and by offering goodness instead. At this point, we are assured that God will provide us a blessing. Our God is a gracious, loving God who longs to shower on his children rewards for

153

Christ-like living. As you incorporate this 1 Peter principle into your life, get ready for God's blessing, because it is certain to come!

Compare the characteristics of 1 Peter 3:8-9 to the characteristics of a defensive marriage. As you examine the following chart, look for the areas that can use the greatest amount of focus in your marriage.

The Cooperative Marriage Partner	The Defensive Marriage Partner
1. Exhibits harmony (unity) even when there are differences.	1. Insists that there must be sameness of thoughts and preferences.
2. Is sympathetic to the spouse's needs and feelings.	2. Wants foremost to be understood.
3. Has a companionlike, brotherly love.	3. Has an adversarial outlook and behavior.
4. Seeks to find ways to be kind.	4. Seeks to find ways to be kind to self.
5. Has an aura of humility.	5. Is pride-infested.
6. Responds to evil with patience.	6. Responds to evil with evil.
7. Responds to insults with gentleness.	7. Responds to insults with insults.
8. Looks for ways to give a blessing.	8. Looks for ways to receive a blessing.

11

Let Freedom Ring!

Freedom! The very mention of the word can send chills up and down the spines of Americans. Ask virtually any person on the streets what he or she likes about our country and the answer will quickly center on the liberties afforded to us in our democratic form of government. We were all taught in our school days that the drive for independence was the single most important factor in making our country what it now is. The names of early freedom fighters such as Patrick Henry, George Washington, and Thomas Jefferson evoke thoughts of appreciation and patriotism as we remind ourselves of their struggles to bring liberty to our nation. We have even proclaimed July 4 as a national holiday to celebrate the onset of our national independence. The virtue of freedom is the cornerstone of our American philosophy!

In the same light, if we were asked to state our grievances against the philosophy of government of Iron Curtain countries, we would readily condemn the notion of restricting personal rights and privileges. We would declare that no group of humans has a true right to dictate to others how life absolutely must or must not be lived. By questioning such forms of government, we would be reminding ourselves that citizens deserve an environment that allows and encourages choices and the free exchange of thoughts and ideals.

We would be in one accord with regard to our notions of basic freedoms being a rightful part of our citizenship. But what about our beliefs regarding freedom within the confines of a marriage? Are we equally as enthusiastic in our effort to maintain a sense of unrestraint in the husband-wife union? My experience in marriage counseling tells me that too often the answer to this question is no. A large percentage of our homes have endless rules and regulations. These easily create in mates a feeling of being smothered and entrapped. Sometimes these restrictions are quite obvious (as in the case of the perennially bossy spouse) and at other times the feeling of entrapment is more subtle (as in the case of spouses who feel stuck together because of religious convictions).

In any event, when a lack of freedom is in evidence in a marriage, strife and defensiveness are inevitable. This would be similar to a feeling that could result from living in a country ruled by a dictatorial tyrant.

Defensiveness that is experienced regularly in marital communications is virtually always due to a lack of a feeling of freedom in that household. Some common illustrations of this are:

With a wife, when:

Her husband thinks religious study is for the birds.

He wants to keep an extra-close tab on how she spends every last penny.

He insists that she should take care of the household chores without bugging him.

He lets her know of his disgust whenever she shows her

emotions. It is an unspoken rule that she isn't supposed to get irritated.

He thinks she ought to spend less time on the phone with her friends and family, and he gripes every time the phone rings.

With a husband, when:

His wife doesn't show any understanding for the pressures he has at work.

She complains about little habits of his that are really trivial matters.

She hounds him about being more productive in the way he spends his free time.

She doesn't like the way he conducts himself at socials, and she lets him hear about it.

It's easier for her to find fault in his personality than it is to give praise.

As you can imagine, there are endless ways in which spouses can feel restricted in their marriage. And the more frequently restrictions such as these are communicated, the more frustrations the restricted partners will experience. In order to avoid the defensive patterns that result from such a restrictive atmosphere, it would be beneficial for spouses to incorporate a philosophy of freedom in their homes. Admittedly, offering freedom carries certain risks, but it is the only true path to marital contentment. Let's examine what freedom in marriage entails.

The Common Sense of Freedom

It is a fact that each human being was created by God for freedom. The concept of being created in the image of

157

God (Gen. 1:27) has many ramifications, not the least of which is the fact that each human has been born with a free will. Ultimately, it is up to all individuals to use that free will to determine how life will be pursued. We thrive best when we are able to exercise our God-given privilege to make our own independent choices. Therefore, when two adults come together in any kind of interaction, they have the greatest chance for relational success when each recognizes the other's privilege of free will.

Fortunately, when God created us with a free will, he was wise enough to also offer us a perfect plan that would lead to a life of fulfillment. He didn't just create us and then send us on our way with no instruction or guidance. Just as a master craftsman will offer instructions to the users of his fine wares, so does God offer teaching to us in the art of caring for ourselves and our relationships. And God's perfect teaching is that we first come to know and understand his love for us (on a free-will basis) to the extent that we earnestly *desire* to become committed to him. Then, within this teaching, he desires that we come to freely comprehend how the marital commitment can be an earthly, experiential picture of the love that exists between God and his family (those who have chosen to call him Father).

When we recognize that he gives us both freedom and instructions regarding patience, submission, and fidelity, we can commit to the Christian way of marriage not out of a sense of pure duty but out of a heart of thankfulness. We are under no obligation to follow his plans, yet we can recognize the positive consequences that will come once we willfully choose to do so.

What does all this mean in terms of the way we will conduct our marital communications? It means that, if God has decided to offer us the gift of free will in our lives, we would be consistent if we came to a similar decision to recognize the free will that our spouse possesses. No spouse has the right to assume an authority position over the other, dictating what that mate must or must not do. Rather, it would be consistent with God's design for each spouse to recognize that the mate should have a choice in how he or she will personally respond to God's instructions. Suggestions, but no dictations, can be offered.

Galatians 5:1 states, "It was for freedom that Christ set us free; therefore keep standing firm and do not be subject again to a yoke of slavery." This thought is echoed in 1 Peter 2:16 which says, "Act as free men, and do not use your freedom as a covering for evil, but as bondslaves of God." (More will be given on this verse later.) As spouses acknowledge the freedom bought for them on the cross by Jesus Christ, they will then honor the freedom of their partner to exercise personal choices.

The Implications of Freedom in Marriage

When one spouse recognizes the privilege of the other spouse to be a free person, it means that each mate will recognize that the other has been given the right by God to choose how he or she will act, speak, feel, behave, think, or believe. It means that each spouse is under no restraints of having to live according to any set agenda for marriage. It means that each spouse is free to choose exactly how much commitment will be given to the marital vows. There are no obligations a spouse must first meet, and there are no regulations to which a spouse is legalistically bound. Life is to be lived with all options open.

Sounds risky, doesn't it! Now, as I said before, don't get the idea that I am advocating the concept of an "anything goes" philosophy.

The point is that no human being has the ultimate right of choosing for another how that person will live. While God gives authority to various people, he gives no human the right to make life's most personal decisions for another. (Authority is given for the sake of organization, not

159

control.) In other words, all people are free to be what they will choose to be, and they are also free to experience the consequences that those choices will bring. Only after individuals recognize their privilege and responsibility to make their own choices can they feel commitments at the deepest level. (Freedom doesn't mean there are no commitments. We are all committed to something.) As we choose various beliefs and commitments from a position of free will, as opposed to obligation, those beliefs and commitments take on greater meaning.

A good illustration of a person who experienced freedom is found in Luke 15. Because of this experience he found his way to a life of fulfillment. This illustration is commonly known as the parable of the prodigal son. In this familiar story, the son seeks and obtains his full freedom from the father. Upon receiving his freedom, he proceeds to find out for himself what life is like on the other side. Finding it eventually to be unsatisfactory, he returns (freely) to his father to recommit himself to the father's service. He doesn't make his commitment under compulsion, but out of desire. You can imagine that once he returned home under free will, he had a true spirit of cooperation and love.

In the meantime, his elder brother disagreed with the acceptance the father had for this son, so he rebuked the father. Of course, you know the father's reply. He wanted the elder brother to recognize that this prodigal son may have temporarily abused his freedom, but ultimately it was this gift of freedom that led to a deep sense of family appreciation and devotion.

In the same light, marriage partners may be reluctant to establish an atmosphere of freedom in their homes because of the possibility of something going wrong. And yet, if spouses are of the same mind as the elder brother, who held strictly to rules and regulations, discord is guaranteed. We would do better to imitate the father's attitude. Notice that when freedom is offered in a marriage, other gifts accompany it:

Unconditional acceptance is given.

Trust is offered, along with a "stamp of confidence."

Partners recognize that neither is superior in worth to the other, but that both are loved equally by God.

The couple that sets an atmosphere of freedom in their home has a high probability of success, because the gifts of acceptance, trust, and worth are very appealing. By injecting these things in the relationship, each partner becomes more attractive to the other. A sense of magnetism can occur because of the joy that is inherent in these gifts.

The Risk of Freedom

So far, the concept of freedom in marriage sounds good. No one wants to be imprisoned in a marriage. But we must recognize that with the offering of freedom there can be problems.

Case Example

June had been married for twenty-three years to a man who had a poor concept of family life. To be blunt, he was insensitive and uncaring in his manner of relating with her. And, to top it off, he had a serious drinking problem. Every night when he came home from work he would park himself in front of the TV with a drink in his hand, getting up only to fix himself another drink. June tried every trick in the book to try to get her husband to become more involved in the lives of the family members. She would talk calmly to him, sometimes yell at him, plead and beg, but she was never able to make this man understand his need to be a more responsible husband and father. He was just too stubborn.

When I suggested to June that she give her husband the freedom to choose how he would live, she was at first bewildered. "But I can't stand the way he is! How can I in good conscience give him the freedom to be something that I detest?" My reply was this: "Notice how successful your efforts have been so far in trying to *force* your husband to change, and then think through the notion of freedom." June then realized that, by trying to fit her husband into her mold, she was only helping him become more resistant and she was driving herself into complete turmoil. She concluded that no matter how right she was, she should let him choose to make his own decisions, even if it meant he made the wrong ones.

When freedom is offered in marriage, there is always the possibility that one or both of the mates will abuse it. Just as we have citizens in our free country who choose to act in a totally irresponsible way, so it is in marriage. In such cases we can at least hold on to the hope that the consequences that accompany poor choices will be a motivation to prompt the individual to consider other courses of action. And, in fact, we can be glad that we have a God who has set into motion just such a system of positive and negative consequences for the choices we make. While he doesn't dictate to us how we should live, he gives us the incentive of potential fulfillment in life if we stay with his promises, and he allows us to struggle with defeats when we stray. In June's case, she held on to the hope that her husband would eventually realize for himself the futility of his ways and be prompted to change.

So, in essence, when freedom is offered in marriage, it is predictable that anything could happen. There is a chance that a marriage partner will adopt the attitude that he or she is free to live in a totally irresponsible way. But just as God took the risk of offering free will to each human, so are we to follow his lead. We can offer freedom in marriage, knowing that the consequences of choices can motivate mates to ultimately decide for themselves what the most profitable lifestyle really is.

This leads us to a major thought. That is, if a spouse is going to successfully lead the life of a Christian husband or wife, it necessitates him or her accepting the burden of

162

figuring out why it is a good idea to follow the Bible's directives. Success in marriage will not come to the person who is living right merely for the sake of following the rules and regulations. Likewise, success will not come to the person who is living right simply because someone else told him or her what had better be done. Success in marriage comes only when each spouse takes the opportunity personally to think through God's plan of salvation and his plan for the Christian life, and then each makes that plan a part of his or her value system because of a desire to make it work. Commitment to marriage based on a personal desire to freely follow God's plan for our lives is the key to true harmony. No one can make this commitment for another person. The choice to commit to God's plan is a personal issue that cannot be forced.

Because of the risk involved in this approach, married couples are more motivated to work hard to create a pleasantness in their personalities. That is, if I am going to take the chance of offering my mate freedom, and if I am truly serious about wanting to have a harmonious marriage, then I will need to be highly motivated to make absolutely sure that my mate is given good reasons for wanting to be committed to our marriage. In offering my mate freedom to be who he or she is, I am automatically assuming a greater personal responsibility in the outcome of the marriage. There will be a realization of my need to be a positive factor in the marriage, thus feeding my mate's desire to reciprocate.

I remember talking with one wife about letting go of her demands on her husband and concentrating more on shaping herself into the right mold of a Christian wife. She replied, "But I'm really not sure my husband will make any efforts with me!" My reply to her was, "If you assume your husband won't cooperate with you, you'll probably get what you are looking for. The truth is that you can't *make* your husband do anything. That's why I'm encouraging you to focus your energies onto yourself." I went on to explain to her that, as long as humans have a sinful nature in them, letting go of one's spouse will always be a risk. The partner's sin nature cannot be controlled by a spouse who tries to live life for the partner. Yet it is encouraging to note that we each can choose to live our lives in such a pleasant way that we will influence our mates to make a similar choice of acting pleasantly.

At this point, it would be helpful to underscore two ideas: (1) When freedom is offered it doesn't mean that opinions are withheld. A spouse can still find tactful ways of sharing thoughts and feelings without giving orders. (2) If, after receiving freedom, a spouse insists on making immoral and unbiblical decisions (such as the decision to be repeatedly abusive or adulterous), the partner is under no compulsion to remain in that situation at the risk of being harmed either psychologically or physically.

Romans 14:12 states, "Each one of us shall give account of himself to God." It may be risky to offer freedom to one's mate, but think of it this way: If I'm going to busy myself thinking about what my spouse ought to be thinking and doing, who is going to be in charge of keeping my own mind in tune with the Lord?

The Balance for Freedom

Let's go back and pick up on a verse that has been previously mentioned. First Peter 2:16 tells us: "Act as free men, and do not use your freedom as a covering for evil, but use it as bondslaves of God." In this writing, Peter acknowledges the need of each person to feel free, and yet he also recognizes that, rather than using freedom in an abusive way, it is possible to choose (in freedom) to have the attitude of a bondslave. It is this attitude that takes the danger out of freedom. If husbands and wives can adopt the attitude of being bondslaves of God and then bondslaves of each other, success in marriage is assured.

164

Exactly what is the bondslave attitude? In the days of the New Testament writings, bondslaves were common. A bondslave was an individual who, as a free person, specifically chose to act in a slave's capacity for a highly respected individual. Nothing was done to keep the bondslave in subjection to the master, yet the bondslave maintained the position of servant out of sheer desire. But there were no strings attached. Choice was the ingredient that separated a bondslave from a regular slave.

You can quickly imagine what the bondslave attitude can do to a husband-wife team. Spouses can have this attitude of being locked into each other, not out of compulsion, but out of desire. When husbands and wives become slavishly committed to God and consequently to the marriage, a new meaning can come to the word *responsibility*. Rather than living with a sense of duty toward each other, a preference for responsible love prevails. Having an undying love and devotion for God, spouses can choose to cling to their marital vows not because "it's what we're supposed to do," but because they want to show honor to him by living in his love. When this occurs, one's Christian reasoning process rather than some stiff list of regulations is in control.

Case Example

Stan and Jackie began their marriage with a high level of devotion to each other. They had a deep love for each other and, besides, they had both been taught that marital commitment was something they were supposed to believe in. But as the years went by, their sense of burning love waned. They came to exhibit defensiveness in their communication styles and consequently experienced the anger and self-esteem problems that result from defensiveness. As the temperament of their marriage changed, their reasons for remaining husband and wife changed. Rather than clinging to each other because of a burning love, they stayed together only because divorce just wasn't an option.

Once they came to my office I encouraged them to seek other reasons for sticking with their marriage. I told them, "Actually, divorce is an option since it is so easy to attain in our courts now. So, technically speaking, you don't have to stay together. I'll share my bias with you by saying that I don't like the option of divorce at all, so I'd prefer that you not go that route. But I'd like to see if we could find another motivation for your commitment to the marriage that doesn't make you feel imprisoned."

When I said this to Stan and Jackie, they both agreed that divorce truly wasn't even a preference for them. So with that in mind, we proceeded to spell out what their preference really was. They both came to similar conclusions. Stan said he wanted to be kind and gentle, and Jackie added that she wanted to have patience and an understanding heart. I then responded, "If you genuinely desire these traits, would you each agree to slavishly pursue them, using that desire as your motivator?" They both agreed that they would. Later Stan told me that, after he recognized that he could commit to being consistent in his role as husband not out of duty but of a servant's heart, his efforts took on new depth and meaning.

A bondslave of marriage is one who recognizes that bitterness, selfishness, defensiveness, and criticism are options that can be pursued, but that these are such poor choices that he or she chooses to refrain from giving in to them. Rather, the marital bondslave, strongly believing in the concept of a harmonious marriage, works fervently to inject the traits of love, joy, and patience into marital communications. These things become a personal goal rather than a duty of drudgery.

The Ultimate Bondslave

We can know that the bondslave attitude is part of God's will for us because it was the very attitude reflected in the life of Jesus Christ. Philippians 2:3-8 explains this so well:

Do nothing from selfishness or empty conceit, but with humility of mind let each of you regard one another as more important than himself; do not merely look out for your own personal interests, but also for the interests of others. Have this attitude in yourselves which was also in Christ Jesus, who, although He existed in the form of God, did not regard equality with God a thing to be grasped, but emptied Himself, taking the form of a bondservant, and being made in the likeness of men. And being found in appearance as a man, He humbled Himself by becoming obedient to the point of death, even death on a cross.

We can rest assured that while the Bible teaches Christians to have the bondslave attitude, we are not being asked to do something that Jesus Christ has not already done. With him as our inspiration and our perfect example, we can determine to strive for Christ-likeness by following his lead. Throughout the pages of the gospel accounts, we read that he had a certain positive stubbornness about him. That is, he was unwavering in his efforts to show gentleness and acceptance to the people who approached him. He did nothing under compulsion, but did everything out of a love that was more profound and deeper than any of us can imagine. When he had the chance to be bossy or controlling, he was cooperative. When he had the option to condemn, he was accepting. When he had the excuse to quit, he kept on going. He slavishly kept himself to the task of following God's will for his life on this earth. Nothing could stop him, because of his overwhelming dedication to his mission.

In the same way, husbands and wives can adopt this spirit. We have been given the perfect example to follow, and we can proceed with the belief that his way is best.

Freedom and Structure

As you can tell, when freedom is offered in marriage, commitment can still be pursued. Some people mistakenly assume that freedom means a lack of structure and accountability. But, in truth, it means a presence of choices. When freedom is offered in marriage, spouses are given the opportunity to choose for themselves how they will live. We can choose the bondslave attitude or we can choose some other approach to marriage.

Actually, when all is said and done, every person will be tied down to some form of structure. Even chaos (the lack of regulation) is a form of structure. And if people fail to exercise their God-given privilege to choose how their lives will be structured, then they will be prone to becoming involuntarily enslaved by an undesirable lifestyle. Second Peter 2:19 tells us, "For by what a man is overcome, by this he is enslaved."

With this in mind, after an atmosphere of freedom is established in the marriage and after the husband and wife agree to a bondslave's attitude toward God and toward each other, *then* the effort to establish communication guidelines will be successful. Plans can be made that will lead the couple to harmonious attitudes and behaviors. Safeguards can be discussed that will bring security to the relationship. Rules can be reestablished and followed, not by decree but by agreement. As a result, the efforts to have harmony will be accomplished from a relaxed rather than from a tense frame of mind.

12

Following the
Original Game Plan

It's always enjoyable and amusing to listen to engaged couples talk of their future with each other. The most notable trait that most of them share is an endless enthusiasm and excitement about their prospects. If you ask them to share their thoughts about their upcoming marriage (and it doesn't take much prodding), they will gladly explain how they have made plans to create an atmosphere of openness and acceptance in their home. They will tell of their intentions to be patient and loving toward each other. And they will already have committed themselves to handle conflicts with reasoning and objectivity. They have it all figured out!

But you and I know that, as time marches on, many couples tend to lose that rosy vision once they actually get into the grind of living with each other's quirks and flaws that just won't disappear. In fact, most of us have even heard couples bemoan the fact of their early naiveness and idealism, saying that they wished they had been more grounded in reality when they first entered marriage.

I'm reminded of one particular couple who, in moments of frustration, would rhetorically ask themselves, "Why couldn't we see our problems coming before we were married? Were we that blind?" In essence, they had dismissed the enthusiasm of their early days by assuming that it just wasn't possible to have the happiness they had once thought could be theirs.

What happens to couples who lose their zest and develop a more sour outlook toward their future? Why do couples get bogged down in petty problems that would have been handled with ease during their times of courtship and high romance? Actually, the answers to these questions can be many and varied, depending on the personalities involved and the circumstances leading to the decision for marriage. Yet, I have found a common key to why couples lose their feeling of optimism in marriage: they have lost sight of their original marital goals. They have been sidetracked by the day-to-day distractions of trying to mesh two separate personalities, to the extent that little focus is given to the overall purpose and direction of the marriage. They are unable to see the forest for the trees.

In order for a marriage to have sustained growth and happiness, a couple must keep their eyes fixed on the overall goal for marriage. There must be a game plan devised and adhered to with regularity. And when the humdrum routine of daily matters sets in and creates a feeling of stagnation, couples will do well to remind themselves of their game plan in order to steer themselves back onto their original course.

Proverbs 29:18 states, "Where there is no vision, the people are unrestrained" (mistranslated as "the people perish" in the King James Version). This tells us that people who do not fix their eyes onto a purposeful plan will be prone to having a lifestyle characterized by chaos and uncertainty. Applied to marriage, we can assume that couples who have no sense of vision for their relationship will be prone to an endless succession of unpredictable and undesirable circumstances.

Couples can successfully maintain a goal orientation in marriage if they will do two things: (1) Have an in-depth understanding of God's plan for marriage, and (2) Commit themselves to specific daily tasks that will keep them attuned to the overall plan.

Case Example

When Tom and Linda look back on the first ten or so years of their marriage, they shake their heads and say something like, "It's a wonder that we stayed together for that long." They had been married in a church wedding when they were in their early twenties and just out of college. Both had a passing knowledge of God's will for marriage, but it was not anything that stimulated much thought in either of them. During the first three or four years, their relationship moved along somewhat smoothly, although neither would claim that they had a spectacular thing going. And then, as time wore on, they began to drift further and further apart. Their in-depth communications became almost nonexistent. They didn't particularly enjoy each other's company. The number of squabbles began to rise and, eventually, they became more intense. So by the time they celebrated their tenth anniversary, they were both questioning whether they should keep plugging away at a dead marriage.

During this low time of disillusionment Tom became acquainted with a minister who really challenged his thinking. He distinctly remembers the minister saying, "God has a plan for your life and it is up to you to discover that plan and live within it." When he heard those words, Tom remarked to himself that he really didn't know God's plan for his life. So logically, he concluded that this lack of understanding was at the very heart of his unhappy home life. With the minister's guidance, he began to discover God's game plan. He began to acknowledge how God created him out of his love for him. And he began to realize for the first time in his life that, as he learned to know and live God's love, it could make a vast difference at home. Tom now shares, "It was only after I came to terms with God's design for my life that I was able to get a feel for what I was supposed to be doing in my marriage. That occurred eight years ago and my only regret is that I didn't have a sense of direction for my life sooner."

No couple will find true harmony in marriage until they find their position in God's overall design. We humans were not placed on this earth by means of some freakish collision. We were each given life by God the Creator, and we were each made for relationships, with him and with others. As we find our niche in God's world, a sense of purpose can come into our lives, guiding us in all aspects of living, and particularly in marriage.

Let's take a close look at God's plan for men and women as it relates to marriage, and then let's examine ways to make that plan come alive!

God's Plan for Husbands and Wives

In order to comprehend God's plan for marriage, it would be beneficial if we would consider why God originally decided to give us life. There is an old folk tale about how God was sitting all by himself in heaven one time feeling lonely. And because of those feelings of isolation, he decided that he would create the world and populate it with people. The story goes on to explain how God gained much happiness in the planning and making of the world. And it explains how God finally relieved himself of his lonely feelings on the day that mankind was formed from the dust of the earth. The story assumes that he made you and me because of his need for companionship.

I suppose this type of story is a fun way of explaining how our lives came into being. But it couldn't be further from the truth! God is no sad, isolated figure who needs the company of humans to make him feel complete. God is a totally sufficient, self-sustaining being. He is perfection itself. He does not need you or me in order that he might thrive.

Actually, God created you and me for the sole purpose of pouring his love into us, thereby making his love more complete than it already was. Before the beginning of time God carefully designed a blueprint that would allow him the privilege of offering his love on a free will basis to anyone who would choose to receive it. And when he designated mankind as the ones with whom he would share this love, he also gave them all the capacity to give and receive love among themselves. We can understand God's design for our lives when we see that we were created first and foremost to be recipients of his love.

Within the overall plan of sharing his love with humans, God created the institution of marriage. He knew that if we humans could have the positive experience of sharing love with our own kind, we would much more likely be able to comprehend the love he has to offer us. And by designating marriage a special, exclusive kind of relationship, it could provide us with an experiential illustration of his special and exclusive love for each of us. God's design for marital and family love was brought about for the purpose of drawing each of us closer to him. That is, as we are able to experience love on the human level, our ability to know love on the spiritual level is enhanced.

In order to better conceptualize this idea, think of how life was for Adam when he was first created. He was perfect, which meant that he had happiness and contentment, as he familiarized himself with his garden home. But God knew that Adam could understand the idea of his love better if he had a companion who was complementary to himself, someone with whom he could share intimacy and closeness. So, because of his desire to give Adam a greater comprehension of love, God gave Adam the gift of a wife, Eve. And we can readily surmise that, as Adam and Eve grew in their love and contentment with each other in their perfect world, they were able to share an increasing appreciation for their Creator who made them with the capacity for love.

As we come to understand that God placed us on the earth, first, to know his love, and second, to share it in human relations, our ability to follow his directives for our lives comes alive. Things make sense. We can understand that God wishes for husbands and wives to share traits such as respect, gentleness, and kindness, because those traits enable us to better know the love for which we were created. And knowing about God's plan for our lives can help us understand why we are taught to be faithful and pure in our marriages. Such teachings are consistent with the faithfulness and purity of his love. As we channel all our behaviors through the concept of living in order to better grasp God's love, we gain a sense of purpose in our relationships that sustains our efforts.

Now I'll admit that there are skeptics who will say, "It's all well and good to think about how God desires to give his love to humans. But let's be honest. We don't live in the same paradise that Adam and Eve once did. Today's modern world is so infected by selfish, insensitive people that it really isn't possible to experience the kind of love intended for us by God."

When I hear such skepticism I realize that there is some truth to what they say. After all, sin *has* stained our world and has caused each of us to lose the full perspective of our reason for existence. In fact, there really are many people who offer nothing but roadblocks when we make the effort to live in God's love. In our modern world, it actually *can* be easier to give up the notion of finding one's place in God's perfect design.

But there is one major fact that can put this skepticism to rest. Jesus Christ has enabled the human race to get back to the original design outlined for mankind by God. Though we have stained God's plans with our sins, thereby alienating ourselves from him and his perfect blueprint, Jesus Christ paid the price for our sins by his death on the cross. By claiming him as our Savior, our go-between with God, we can become restored to God and have a regenerated ability to follow his design. Further, Jesus Christ reminded us through his teachings how we can live in God's love by making our love for one another predominant in our lives. In fact, when a man once asked Jesus to name the greatest of all commandments, he underscored the gist of our existence by stating:

> "You shall love the Lord your God with all your heart, and with all your soul, and with all your mind." This is the great and foremost commandment. And a second is like it, you shall love your neighbor as yourself. (Matt. 22:37-39)

So, as we commit ourselves to Jesus Christ and closely follow his instructions, we can expect to live in a loving way in the human arena, in a way that will cause us to comprehend love in the spiritual realm, between ourselves and God.

The Implications for Marriage

Marriage is such a key factor in knowing and experiencing the love of God that the Bible actually draws a parallel between a husband's love for his wife and Christ's love for his church. For instance, several times in the Book of Revelation we are given a futuristic picture of Jesus Christ taking into marriage his bride, the church. (For an example of this, see Rev. 19:7-9; 21:1-9.) And, in the most famous biblical passage on the subject of marriage, the analogy is drawn of husbands relating to wives as Christ relates to his people:

> Husbands, love your wives, just as Christ also loved the church and gave Himself up for her; that He might sanctify her, having cleansed her by the washing of water with the word, that He might present to Himself the church in all her glory, having no spot or wrinkle or any such thing; but that she should be holy and blameless (Eph. 5:25-27).

Marriage is no old-fashioned, outdated institution that

175

has little or no significance (as some of our more liberal-minded thinkers will tell us). Rather, marriage plays a key role in helping individuals know the essence of love. And, as we seek to sustain our marriages in a pure and undefiled manner, we can truly know love. We will want to make the most of our marital relations, not because we're supposed to get married and stay married, but because we understand it to be a central cog in God's overall plan of communicating his love for us.

With this in mind, let's examine several key points that will help each of us maintain a sense of purpose in our marriages.

1. Marriage is meant to have an open, sharing atmosphere. When a husband and wife realize that marriage is meant to be a relationship that enables them to know the essence of love, they will have a heart's desire to allow each partner to see inside the other. They will recognize that openness is essential. They will agree that marriage involves more than just living in the same house, sharing meals, sharing the bedroom, and bringing up kids. There will be efforts to create a sense of belonging and of appreciation of one another. Notice some of the ways this can be accomplished:

Spouses can find ways to daily share compliments regarding routine matters.

They can inject comments of warmth and tenderness regularly.

Even sour feelings can be declared, but it will be done objectively and with a constructive purpose.

They will share fun activities together. Laughter will be present in the home.

When insecurities are felt, there will be a willingness to share them.

Both partners will be on the lookout to find ways to

make the mate feel more at ease when they are together.

Joint devotional times will be a part of their daily routine.

When a problem in the marriage is brought to a spouse's attention, there will be a willingness, even a desire, to hear the opposing point of view.

Nonverbal means of positive regard (eye contact, touching, etc.) will be evident.

There will be an allowance for the fact that personalities will differ.

It is within this atmosphere of open sharing that a feeling of unity between husband and wife can occur. By having a track record of showing interest in each other and in allowing one another to know the innermost parts of each other, spouses will form a bond that defies adequate description. They will share a distinction in their marriage that sets their relationship apart from the more superficial nature of most of their other relationships. Perhaps they will be able to echo the words of the elderly gentleman who said, "I can't exactly tell you what it is that I like most about my wife. But I can tell you this: I always know that she's on my team and she wants to make life good for me."

2. Marriage is where giving occurs. Ephesians 5:1 tells us quite simply to be "imitators of God." So naturally, it is incumbent on us to study his nature and follow his lead. And when we identify the various atttributes of our Maker, we very quickly discover that he is the ultimate gift giver. Consider the following verses that describe the giving nature of God:

And the Lord God fashioned into a woman the rib which He had taken from the man, and brought her to the man (Gen. 2:22).

In Him we have redemption through His blood, the forgiveness of our trespasses, according to the riches of His grace, which He lavished upon us (Eph. 1:7-8).

For God so loved the world that He gave His only begotten Son . . . (John 3:16).

My peace I give to you (John 14:27).

It is clear that it pleases God to give. In fact, it is through giving that he receives joy.

Do you remember what you were like as a child at Christmas time? As I recall my early days, I remember vividly being so excited on Christmas Eve that I could hardly sleep waiting for morning to come. Opening the presents (*my* presents) was the one and only thing my mind could focus on. Would I get that new bike I wanted? How about the games that would be there? Maybe some new shirts? Now, as I greet Christmas each year, it's funny how my feelings are different. Rather than being worried about what I will receive, my greatest joy comes in what I can give to my own children. What a thrill to see those faces light up at the sight of a new doll or a new dress! I'm all smiles when I know my gifts have made someone happy. The appreciative hug and the "Thank you, Daddy" make it all worthwhile.

Most parents will share the same feeling about giving gifts to their kids. But it is odd that, in our marriages, particularly in the area of emotional issues, we still crave very much to be on the receiving end of things. Too often there is a "What's in it for me?" attitude among mates. As an example, one spouse may complain to the other that there is not enough love or attention given. Or one mate may bemoan the fact that he or she is not given enough due consideration in decisions that are made. "What about me?" is the point of view expressed most often. (I'm not suggesting that we never assert our needs. My focus here is on one's overall mind-set.)

If marriages are to carry out their purpose as outlined

by God, giving will be dominant. Spouses will be willing to give in a wide variety of matters, such as understanding, kindness, compliments, constructive suggestions, time, encouragement, and patience. Through giving the spouses will be able to express the love that is of God. By extending ourselves in this manner, we are imitating him.

Now, I know there are some who are reluctant to replace their desire to receive with the desire to be a giver. As I discussed the idea of being givers in marriage with one couple, the wife looked hesitant. So I asked her to share her apprehensions with me. She said, "As you were talking about giving, the thought crossed my mind that I may decide to give to my husband, but he may not feel the urge to make the same decision. I'm not sure if it would feel all that good." I replied that she was correct in assuming that giving is more pleasurable when *both* mates are seeking ways to extend themselves to one another. And yet, even if there are times when giving is one-sided, my preference is to pursue it still. After all, people who give can create a warmth in themselves and the benefit is felt. It is better for one mate to be a giver than for neither to give.

3. Marriage partners will seek to bring out the best in each other. A couple once complained to me that they had lost the love that had existed in the early years of their marriage. When I asked how this happened, they both shrugged their shoulders and said they didn't really know. But as we proceeded in our conversation, the answer to the question became obvious. It took very little prodding before one of them would toss a sarcastic criticism toward the other. And I heard them both explain how an atmosphere of pessimism permeated their home. Each one seemed intent on outdoing the other in giving gripes and negative remarks. Within such a style of communication it was easy to see that they definitely brought out the worst in each other. Each was so overwhelmed by the other's negativism that self-control was almost impossible.

God's original game plan for man and wife was one which was meant to bring an upbeat atmosphere to life. When God gave Adam his wife, Eve, she was meant to be a helpmate. That is, she was to be a partner for life who would be highly instrumental in helping her husband know the contentment of living within God's design. Even though Adam was perfect when they married, she was given to him in wedlock in order that he might be able to share his finest qualities in ways that would not have been possible with his animal companions. As Adam and Eve were able to express their love for each other, they had a full understanding of the breadth of majesty created in them.

Whether or not we are aware of it, each marital partner exerts an influence over the other spouse. Each has the ability to either squelch or enhance the mate's inner strengths, depending on the stimulation given to one another. For example, a spouse can bring out cynicism in a mate by being rude and uncaring, or a spouse can elicit warmth from a mate by being attentive and understanding. Since we were created by God as interdependent beings, one can become an asset to one's mate when a concerted effort is made to offer consistently positive behavior. First Thessalonians 5:11 echoes this theme as it states, "Therefore encourage one another, and build up one another."

4. *Marriage is guided by a sense of commitment.* When we have an in-depth comprehension of God's purpose for marriage, we can recognize that a sense of commitment is inherent in his plan. When God instituted marriage, he didn't say, "Let's see how this goes and, if it doesn't work, we'll come up with something different." He intended marriage to be an experience of one person sharing love with another as long as they are given life. Just as God's love is not temporary, he desires that we not pursue an

180

endless succession of temporary marital loves. By seeking to have a lifelong commitment to one another, we are imitating his eternal love for us.

God's commitment toward us is so strong that he chooses to offer himself to us in spite of our sins. Though each of us at some time in our lives has shaken our fists at him in rebellious defiance, he has chosen to pursue us with his love. While we are weak and inconsistent in our devotion to him, he is tenacious in his effort to keep us by his side. In fact, this point is most vividly illustrated by the fact that Jesus Christ offered himself as a sacrifice on our behalf. He is the ultimate illustration of the commitment God has toward us. It was with this understanding that the apostle Paul wrote the words, "Husbands, love your wives, just as Christ also loved the church and gave himself up for her" (Eph. 5:25). And within the same context Paul wrote, "Let the wife see to it that she respect her husband" (Eph. 5:33).

Since the commitment of the Lord is so powerful that it caused him to pursue us in spite of our rebellious nature, a couple who is living within God's game plan will seek to have this same stick-to-it mentality. This doesn't mean that once couples become wed they are to remain together legalistically merely to satisfy a Christian principle. Rather, it means that individuals with this tenacious sense of commitment will seek to do anything reasonable and possible to inject love into the home. It is interesting to note some of the implications of a couple's strong commitment to each other:

They will regularly remind each other of their valuable status.

Fair treatment toward one another will come as second nature.

Even when gaps appear in their relationship, efforts

will be made to be constructive in seeking resolutions.

Each partner will see him/herself as an initiator of love, as opposed to being one who waits to be loved first.

Forgiveness will be offered with no strings attached.

Marriage will be considered as a sacred institution and persistent efforts will be made to keep it thriving.

Sexual infidelity won't be an option.

There will be a willingness to stand by one's mate through thick and thin.

To summarize, we can each gain a sense of direction in marriage when we go back to the original plans for marriage, seeking to make it pertinent to our modern-day world. While we have many current philosophies that seek to distort and water down the beauty of the Christ-centered home, we can come to the conclusion that no new philosophy has been able to match the timeless truths presented in God's design. The key to making his plan work in our homes is (1) powerful awareness of what God is willing to do for us as we follow his will, and (2) a persistent concentration on the task of translating his will into our daily routines.

13

Keeping Pride in Check

So far we have discussed several factors involved in overcoming defensive communications. With an understanding of the problem and a concentration on the task, new and more effective ways of relating are possible for the couple mired in a rut of resistance. But no matter how much knowledge is gained, and no matter how much concentration is made, defensiveness will not be conquered until one major roadblock is removed—the roadblock of pride.

In our modern culture pride has become a word that often has positive connotations. For example, workers are encouraged to take pride in the jobs they do. Athletes are encouraged to be proud of their abilities. Parents know what it is like to glow with pride when one of their children excels in a performance. At election time we are told to take pride in our country. These examples and many more illustrate that pride represents a feeling of respect, contentment, or satisfaction toward the object of one's emotion. In this sense, pride can have healthy results.

But there is another side of pride that we are to avoid at

all costs, if our desire is to create harmony in relationships. It is the pride of arrogance (either obvious or subtle). It is the pride that causes a person to close him/herself off from another who might not be considered worthy of attention. It is the pride that causes one to rarely admit flaws or errors, assuming instead an aura of resistance and even of condescension. This kind of pride is at the very heart of defensive communication. This kind of pride is rebuked in Proverbs 8:13, which states, "The fear of the Lord is to hate evil; Pride and arrogance and the evil way, and the perverted mouth, I hate." In other words, it may be fine for us to have a pride that manifests itself in a modest sense of self-respect and satisfaction with our position in life, but pride can be quite negative if it becomes exaggerated to the extent that it undermines one's ability to relate lovingly with others.

In its extreme form, pride can be defined as an exaggerated preoccupation with one's own importance and desires. It implies an overconcern with one's standing with others and with one's own needs and preferences. It can be exhibited in an open show of arrogance and superiority. Or (as is more often the case) it can be exhibited very subtly in the form of super-sensitivity and the desire to be catered to.

Case Example

Roberta was a woman who would never be described by her friends and acquaintances as being showy or arrogant. She was consistently conservative in her mannerisms. She was not a bossy kind of person, but was perfectly content in playing second fiddle in the various relationships. Yet, in spite of her low-keyed, easy-going ways, Roberta had a problem with pride that caused her to behave defensively quite frequently.

You see, Roberta was the kind of person who could keep her cool as long as her life remained predictable and orderly. And she was able to be friendly and outgoing *as long as* the people in her presence acted correctly. But as soon as she began losing her feeling of control in her social circumstances, Roberta was prone to worrying and fretting. And if her husband or a friend made a suggestion or confrontation (however mild) that offended her, she often would give way to tears and would hide behind a wall of silence. During such moments, she would complain about how she felt unappreciated and used. She was not open to considering feelings and ideas presented to her by others, which might cause her to alter her own set way of thinking and behaving. At the base of it all, it was apparent that Roberta was so mentally and emotionally consumed with her own preferences and desires that it kept her from exhibiting the flexibility and openness that is so necessary in a growing, harmonious relationship.

Think about the various ways pride influences emotions and behaviors. To illustrate, you can be assured that pride is at work whenever you find yourself holding onto grudges, when worry is prominent, when feelings of hurt will not go away, or when there is a refusal to openly share feelings that might cause you to look a little more human. In each of these cases, there is an undercurrent of exaggerated preoccupation with one's own needs and importance. In order to closely identify this kind of pride in yourself, look over the following check list to see if you have experienced some of its signs.

1. A critical mind-set is fairly prominent.
2. It is difficult to accept a point of view different from your own.
3. There is a hesitancy to admit failures.
4. There is a tendency to be controlling and demanding.
5. When you express your point of view, it is done with insistence.
6. Impatience toward another's shortcomings is common.
7. Your feelings are hurt fairly easily.
8. When things don't go your way, you brood and sulk.
9. Unpredictable mood changes are not uncommon.
10. You don't like to stoop to do menial chores.

185

As you might imagine, when marital partners allow themselves to get caught up in such behaviors, defensiveness is a sure result. It is only logical that pride can be a detriment to marital relations, since marriage calls for a consistent giving up of oneself, and since pride is by nature concerned with self. Therefore, in order to take a step away from defensive communications and toward harmony, it will be to our advantage to understand more of the nature of pride, so that steps can be made to keep it in check.

Why Pride Occurs

The reasons for pride's existence in our lives are varied. It can be inbred in us in our childhood, it can stem from insecure feelings, or it can represent a need to be looked up to. Actually though, if we traced pride all the way to its most basic foundation, we would find that it is intricately linked to mankind's natural disposition toward sin. In fact, it played a key role in the onset of the very first sin ever committed.

Take your imagination back once again to those original days when Adam and Eve lived in total perfection. They had absolutely no problems in their communications with each other, because they each inwardly bore the unstained image of God. But at the temptation of Satan, Eve and then Adam decided that they would test God. He had told them to stay away from the Tree of the Knowledge of Good and Evil. That is, they had been commanded by God to let him be the only one to determine right and wrong. If they would simply trust and follow his guidance, they would have an endless reservoir of contentment. But you know what happened. Rather than following the instructions of the Lord, they got caught up with self-importance (pride). They began to feel an exaggerated sense of dignity and they dared to assume that they could outsmart God. So in pride, Adam and Eve deliberately chose to disobey him. (For an account of this, read Gen. 3:1-6.) Pride caused them to consider their own knowledge superior to the Creator's.

Now, it is interesting to note what happened immediately after Adam and Eve chose to pridefully elevate themselves. After sinning, they instantly realized the error of their ways and instinctively went to a defensive maneuver. They felt the need to cover up! Genesis 3:7 tells us: "Then the eyes of both of them were opened, and they knew that they were naked; and they sewed fig leaves together and made themselves loin coverings."

Then, immediately after they covered up before each other, they each tried an evasive defensive maneuver with God. When God questioned Adam about his deed of arrogance, what did he do? He blamed Eve! "It's not my fault, it's my wife's fault!" And when God questioned Eve about her misdeed, what did she do? She blamed the snake. "The devil made me do it!" (see Gen. 3:8-13).

So we see that Adam and Eve went through a quick progression of events. First, they each began to think more highly of themselves than they should. Second, they committed a deed (we don't know exactly what they did) that openly displayed their grandiose feelings about their importance. Third, they made the decision to cover up, both in the physical and the psychological sense. Then finally, they began playing games with each other and with God himself.

The saddest part of this story about Adam and Eve's prideful indulgence of themselves is that this was only the first of many times they behaved in such a way. While they knew they were wrong, they became addicted to self-glorification. So, quite naturally, this problem was passed on to their children and to each successive generation.

This explains why it is so natural for each of us to get sidetracked in our positive communication efforts. As long as we have the prideful tendency to be preoccupied with self, relationships suffer. We are like Adam and Eve in that we each have times in which we allow ourselves to think too highly of ourselves, placing ourselves at the center of the universe.

By understanding how pride was a central factor in mankind's fall into sin, and by realizing that as stained, sinful humans we will have continual struggles with this problem, it is important that we examine how we allow this trait to affect our daily lives. Since pride is at the base of virtually all sins, it is crucial that we identify it and seek ways to overcome it.

With this in mind, let's examine three key factors to be harnessed so that pride can be held in check.

The Desire to Be Superior

Every human being alive (bar none) has inner struggles with feelings of inferiority. This is due in part to our inward realization of our personal imperfections and, in part, to the fact that we started life in a dependent position with built-in deficiencies. Ideally, it would be good if each person would have had strong parental training during the formative years, training that focused on the equality of one human to the next and on the fact that God's love can lift us from our lowly sinful position to one of value and worth.

However, the reality is that most people do not grow up with a clear notion of the meaning of God's love for each individual, nor do we fully think through the concept of equality among all people. We tend to learn very early in life the false notion that one person can become superior to another by way of some performance. Or we learn that one person may gain special favor with authority figures (including God) by learning how to play up to their preferences and desires. In other words, most of us are trained in some form or fashion to get caught up in the man-made game of being superior. It takes little imagination, then, to comprehend how this fuels feelings of pride, since pride is the trait of being preoccupied with one's standing in life.

The drive for superiority has many dimensions. The most obvious manifestation is seen in the person who feels the need to be in charge, or who has to get the last word in, or who exhibits an arrogant disdain for others who do not meet their standard. But there are also more subtle, secretive ways a person may attempt to gain superiority. For example, some spouses know that they are not able to gain the upper hand in arguments by way of forceful speeches, so they go down the low road of using the silent treatment. Some spouses don't use either of these power tactics. They seek superiority by proving their higher position by living a life of pious perfection (and having an accompanying critical mind-set).

Unless we become aware of the popular game of becoming superior, we will be forever mired in inappropriate feelings of pride. We can become so preoccupied with the need to gain a competitive edge over our fellow humans that our sense of cooperation and helpfulness is almost entirely lost. Consequently, there is a need to remind ourselves of the biblical teaching that "God is not one to show partiality" (Acts 10:34). That is, he doesn't think in terms of one person being superior to another; he values each of us equally. Therefore, since God has a belief in the equal value of each individual, then we are wise to accept the same notion.

This means that the striving for superiority can cease. Since we are assured by God himself that we are equally valued by him, the sense of inferiority can be erased, thereby eliminating the need to get caught in the one-up, one-down game.

The Humanistic Foundation for Living

It should be clear by now that enjoying full success and security in marital relationships will occur only as each partner determines to set aside his or her own natural selfish tendencies and to seek, instead, to let God's will permeate their lives.

People who live with excessive pride, however, do the opposite. They assume they have the ability to decide for themselves how life should be lived in order to provide the desired level of security. I recall one woman who rationalized her behavior to me in this way: "I know that the Bible teaches us to be accepting of others even when they make mistakes. But I'm sorry; I just won't accept my husband when he gets in his bad moods. Maybe you'll tell me I'm wrong to hold grudges against him, but that's just the way it is."

This woman was aware that, even in the midst of her difficult marital situation, certain attitudes (as spelled out in the Bible) would be most beneficial. But deliberately disregarding those teachings, she decided to place more stock in her own reasoning. She was attempting to establish a base of security for herself based on her own misguided emotions. For a short while she may have felt satisfied but, in the long course of things, her reasoning is guaranteed to lead her to ruin.

Such a humanistic approach to life can be identified by several key traits.

My rights have first priority. The prideful, humanistic way of thought readily elevates self to the position of highest priority in one's thoughts. While others' needs may at times be considered, self always comes out on top when there is a dilemma regarding who is to be served. One's personal rights are considered in advance of one's personal responsibilities. As an example, think of a husband whose wife is sad because of some difficulties encountered during the day. His first response when he hears of her low feelings is, "I suppose this means that I'll have to go out and get hamburgers again for supper!"

God's ways aren't always the best. When persons seek humanistic ways to solve life's problems, God's ways may or may not be followed, depending on how closely his guidelines suit their desires. People who live with this tendency find it easy to question the teachings of the Lord. They live as if their problems are too different to be helped by following his design. For example, picture a wife who says, "I know the Bible says that wives are to show respect to their husbands, but my husband doesn't treat me right. So I'm excused from that teaching."

Go with the way you feel right now. A basic problem with prideful, humanistic people is the tendency to let the present dominate one's thoughts. Little attention is given to either the past or the future. That is, there may be little sympathy in trying to understand how a series of past events may help create current problems. And there is little effort made to act in the present with a thoughtful eye toward the future. In other words, these people can be so now oriented that there is little perspective of how current actions fit into the breadth of time. To illustrate, imagine a spouse who complains unduly about a mate's social skills. In this instance, there is likely a lack of comprehension of the mate's personal background, and there is little thought given about what such complaints will do to the couple's future.

I'm really a pretty good person. Too often, prideful people think so highly of themselves that there is little, if any, open recognition of their need for changes. In a self-building exercise, these people will firmly believe that the only thing that can keep them from becoming near-perfect is the environment. When this occurs, it is easy to sidestep full responsibilities for personal errors. This is what causes some of them to say to their mates, "The only thing that keeps me from being in control of myself is you!"

The Lack of a True Sensitivity

Sensitivity is a word with a two-edged meaning. We think of a person who is easily hurt as being sensitive. But we also think of one who has a warm, giving nature as being sensitive. It is clear that a person exhibiting a prideful spirit is one who is more likely to live in the first meaning of the word, one who is easily hurt. This person has an abiding concern about self without an equal feel for the emotions of others.

When a self-oriented sensitivity is prominent, the individual is likely to have a "What-will-you-do-for-me?" frame of mind. Relationships are conducted for the sake of what one might receive. Even when giving is done, there is usually a hidden ulterior motive. Spouses with this frame of mind usually show their colors by pouting and becoming irate when an act of kindness is not properly reciprocated.

The key factor that shows whether the second meaning of sensitivity—a giving spirit—is properly at work in one's relationships is the trait of loving others without a primary worry about self's needs. When this occurs, spouses are freed to communicate in many satisfactory ways. Emotions can be openly shared without the fear of causing unwarranted reactions. When disagreements occur, there is not as much of an effort made to prove one's point of view as there is an effort to understand the spouse and to seek mutually satisfying solutions.

The Solution for Pride

Jesus Christ explained the solution for prideful behavior when he said to his disciples:

> If anyone wishes to come after me, let him deny himself, and take up his cross, and follow me. For whoever wishes to save his life shall lose it; but whoever loses his life for my sake shall find it (Matt. 16:24-25).

The key to defeating pride is to take self out of life's driver's seat and to let the Lord take over the controls.

This means that I will acknowledge my inherent weaknesses as a sinner and will therefore cling to the words of Christ for guidance and direction. In humbleness, I will be willing to pray: "Lord, I know that my greatest mistake is in not letting you be my source of strength and stability. Come into my heart and show me your ways. I'm a willing vessel for you."

When we understand pride to be caused initially by an effort to out-think God and then by the tendency to place self first in one's considerations, we can quickly deduce that this problem can be overcome by submission to God's universal law of love and by a willingness to place the needs of others before those of self. If this could be accomplished in a husband-wife relationship, think of the positive results that would be immediately evident.

Each spouse goes to extra lengths to give the other a pleasant day.

Love is expressed via a servant's heart.

Gentleness is dominant in the home atmosphere.

When problems occur, each spouse examines self for solutions.

Forgiveness comes naturally. Grudges are not held.

Communication is open. Secrets are not kept.

Praise is far more prominent than criticism.

Devotion and commitment to God binds the relationship together.

Listening and understanding is at a premium.

Feelings are not easily hurt; rational thinking is in evidence.

Even though each individual (like Adam and Eve) has chosen pride, thereby creating defensiveness, we can be assured that God is willing to forgive our indiscretion and to show us the way back to a fulfilled life. But it is only when we determine to let him be Lord of our lives that his plans will become truly rewarding.

Case Example

Jack came to my office after several years of misery in his home life. He shared how he and his wife had at one time enjoyed a closeness and a deep love for each other. But somewhere along the way his union with her had become broken. As I asked him to share why this occurred, he went into great detail about how he had allowed himself to become almost completely consumed with his own desires and needs. He told me that, in his conversations with his wife, he would constantly worry about her perceptions of him. He seemed to be obsessed with the notion that she owed him her love and allegiance. (Of course, this didn't sit well with her.) And he shared with me how he had become prone to emotional highs and lows, sometimes becoming easily irate while at other times becoming silently tense.

As we discussed his broken marriage, I suggested to Jack that he should examine his feelings of pride. I asked him to spend one week making notes of the times he would become overly preoccupied with himself. When we met the following week, Jack told me that he was utterly amazed with the number of times he would allow his selfish needs and desires to dominate his emotions. In stark honesty, he said, "Les, if I had to live with someone as self-absorbed as I, I think they would have to lock me up in a padded cell. When I truly saw how worried I was about me, I was ashamed."

After Jack's eyes were opened to his pride, he made a major turn-around in his style of communication. No longer consumed with his selfish needs, he felt freed to respond more consistently to his wife's feelings. He found that he had a tremendous ability to buoy her spirits by merely becoming a concerned listener. And whenever his wife would offer him feedback regarding areas to potentially change, he took her thoughts to heart. By humbly setting aside self's preoccupations, Jack learned that he could actually gain the very things he was previously trying to find by being totally self-consumed!

To be sure, a humble spirit is not natural to any of us. This is due to the fact that our fall into sin has caused each of us to have a greater inclination to serve self than to serve others. And since humility involves a sense of modest self-appraisal (as opposed to self-glorification), mak-

194

ing the decision to act humbly takes daily all the concentration we can muster. Yet, once we allow God's nature to permeate our wills and consequently our behavior, we can develop the habit of thinking as he would have us think, thereby placing a greater premium on the needs of others. When we get to this point in our minds we will be able to follow the advice given in Philippians 2:3: "Do nothing from selfishness or empty conceit, but with humility of mind let each of you regard one another as more important than himself."

In practical terms, this means that a husband who seeks to set pride aside will develop a habitual tendency to think of the love God has for his wife, which will prompt him to openly communicate in a caring fashion. Likewise, it means that the wife will have a consuming desire to let God's will guide her communication practices with her husband. She will seek to follow the Lord's guidelines in the flow of everyday interactions.

When we replace pride by humbly considering other's needs before self's needs, it doesn't mean that we will have a disrespect for self. Rather, it means that we will desire to live in his love far more deeply than we will desire to live in our own tendencies. The end result, then, will be a marriage that is upbeat and encouraging. Pleasure will be derived not from what is received, but from what is given.

Part Four

The How To's
of Harmonious Living

14

A Formula for Harmony

Whenever solutions are sought for problems in marital communications, most couples make the mistake of seeking out the how to's first. That is, they try to latch onto some external solutions for their personal woes before first developing solid internal insights into their feelings and behaviors. Magazine articles, popular books, and radio and TV talk shows are quite appealing to the general public because of their tendency to tell us how we can gain happiness in life in just ten easy steps. It's no wonder that we become easily caught in the illusion that, if we will merely follow the formulas set forth by today's experts, life will become a bowl of cherries and relationships will be purely blissful.

Of course, most of us will admit (grudgingly perhaps) that there really is no such thing as an instant cure to all our woes. While we would like to think that our troubles can just vanish by following a bit of good advice, reality tells us that it's not quite that simple.

I'm reminded of the couple who came to my office seeking counseling but with minds of deep skepticism.

They had already worn out six other therapists (at least they were tenacious!), and they weren't very hopeful about anything that I might offer them. Rather than telling them what they should be doing differently in their marriage, I asked them to share with me their own formula for marital success. Very quickly it was apparent that they could readily recite all the good how to's. A lack of knowledge was definitely not their problem. So we decided to focus instead on the reasons why they fell short in their efforts to implement their knowledge. We sought to establish insight first so that the how-to formula could then be followed successfully.

By now you should have enough insight into defensive communications that you will be able to integrate the final thoughts of this book into your lifestyle. The truth is that how-to formulas for success actually can be quite helpful to the individual who has a keen thoughtfulness regarding his or her own personality makeup and purpose in life. We can all use some pertinent suggestions that will give outward evidence to our inner insights.

But before you read the communication suggestions offered in this chapter, let me encourage you to ask the following questions:

Do I have a pretty good idea of the aspects of my communication that need to be refined?

Am I aware of the reasons why I communicate the way I do?

Do I have a working understanding of the way my emotions influence my behavior?

Have I given deep thought to my overall goals in marriage?

Am I guided by a sense of purpose?

Do I have the high level of motivation that will prompt

me to make necessary positive changes in my communications?

If you can answer these questions affirmatively, you will probably be quite successful in your efforts to implement the formula for harmonious communication outlined below.

Following are some practical suggestions that will help build an atmosphere of harmony in your home. Remember, concentration to the task will be vitally important as you choose to interact within these guidelines.

Step 1
Develop a reputation as an encourager

Time after time in my counseling office I have heard couples complain about a prevailing critical spirit in their homes. Husbands and wives frequently share with me the compelling wish that they could have a friendly, happy tone in their marital interactions. They fear that a constant threat of criticism from their spouse can be the kiss of death to the possibility of marital happiness. And they are right! These frustrated couples know that they need encouragement far more than criticism.

Being an encourager (as opposed to being a critic) requires that spouses will have thought through their goals for marriage. Encouraging spouses will have concluded that the marriage should be a relationship that gives a feeling of specialness. Encouragers know that we each have a deep and abiding need to be affirmed, and they will feel privileged to be the one who can be counted on to affirm their marriage partner. They will recognize that they can quickly bring pleasure to an otherwise dreary day by giving a ready smile, by complimenting the mate even in small matters, and by letting the partner know of their commitments to love and happiness. Encouragers understand the impact of a pleasant exchange, and they desire to give a breath of fresh air whenever the opportunity presents itself.

Look over the following items that describe typical encouraging behaviors and examine yourself in comparison.

Encouragers have a knack for saying what they do like as opposed to what they don't like.

They work to understand the moods and quirks of their mates and they seek to adjust their communications accordingly.

Daily they communicate a love and kindness to their mates.

If the mood at home is down, they don't wait for the spouse to change before acting pleasantly. They want to initiate an upbeat mood.

Encouragers like to do small favors without being asked.

They are ready with compliments and give them often.

They are willing to offer a listening ear when their spouse has feelings to share.

The actual steps to becoming an encourager are simple to spell out. The real challenge in being successful in this trait is to be consistent. That's how reputations are formed.

Step 2
Offer acceptance even in disagreements

Have you noticed something? It's easy to accept others when they are acting the way we want them to act. For example, I don't have any problem enjoying the company of one who is friendly and interested in me. But what about the times when we encounter a person who isn't anything close to what we like? And what happens when that person is one's mate? The natural tendency is to ignore and even reject that individual.

But in a relationship that seeks harmony, acceptance is not a factor that comes and goes with performance. Acceptance is offered in the good times and it is offered even when things aren't so great. Harmonizers are spouses who seek to initiate unconditional love for each other. It's not easy, but it can be done.

To illustrate the way unconditional acceptance can be offered, let me share with you how one couple handled their disagreements. This couple realized early in their marriage that their personalities were not exactly of the same mold, so they knew that disagreements would be inevitable. It was merely a fact that they interpreted the world differently. So they each agreed that, when the other would become frustrated, perhaps saying something inappropriate, they would not be shocked. And consequently, they wouldn't try to talk the other out of those sour feelings, nor would they discount the other's unique point of view. Rather, this couple wisely recognized that if they held a rational acknowledgment of their human imperfections, they would be less likely to let their disagreements get blown out of proportion. In other words, before disagreements even occurred, they agreed to accept the inevitability of their likelihood. But guess what? With this frame of mind, they found that they had far less than the average number of disagreements. By allowing for them, they occurred less frequently.

To be sure, it is somewhat risky to accept one another's differences. The risk is that the difference can actually heighten if couples are not careful with such traits as sarcasm or laziness. But when couples have common sense in their understanding of mankind's sinful nature and in their expectations for marriage, they will find that acceptance comes naturally. The result of this attitude is less emotional intensity regarding disagreements and more of a sense of fair play and understanding.

Step 3
Avoid abusing the word *you*

Of all the offensive words that can be spoken by marital partners, the innocent little word *you* has sparked more arguments than all the rest. When a difference of opinion arises or when changes need to be made at home, spouses can almost instinctively unleash a string of thoughts anchored by the word *you*. When this occurs, two results are likely: First, the accusing partner absolves him/herself from any responsibility of problem-solving. Second, the other spouse feels backed into a corner and thereby feels the need to defend him/herself. Needless to say, at that point constructive discussions are rare.

As an alternative, when problems arise and you are wishing to find a pliable resolution, be willing to put yourself (not your partner) on the line. Rather than telling your partner what he or she should do differently, explain out loud how you would like to contribute to the solution. Then see how much more receptive your spouse will be. For instance, rather than saying, "I wish you would be more positive in the way you talk to me," you might try, "I'd like to have more pleasant communications in our home and I'm planning to be more aware of my need to be sensitive and complimentary." By taking this approach, the spouse becomes aware of your feelings about the relationship without feeling pinned down.

This style of communication is called indirect confrontation. The issues calling for change are openly addressed, but the confronted partner does not feel as if the whole burden of change is being placed on his or her shoulders. A sense of cooperation is implied from the beginning of the conversation. In this style of confrontation, an assumption is made that the one who witnesses the spouse declaring a willingness to change will likewise commit to make improvements. This indirect form of confrontation is likely to have more lasting results, because the confronted spouse is left to think personally about the changes that should be made, as opposed to having the confronting spouse think for him or her.

Step 4
Share understanding before offering solutions

Not long ago, a husband was talking with his wife in my counseling office about problems they were having with their children. She was frustrated with him, but he couldn't understand why. So he said, "Honey, I don't know what you're so upset about. I've told you how you should handle our situation at home. What more do you want from me?" The wife looked at him through her tears and said, "I don't want your solutions. I just want you to understand me!"

So often when problems arise in marriage (however great or small), the first tendency of spouses is to offer solutions. Try to recall a recent time when your spouse shared a frustrating experience or an insecure feeling. How did you respond? If you are like most people, you probably started with something like, "Well, maybe it would help if you would . . ." or "Honey, all you need to do is . . ." or "Have you tried . . . ?" Now think about the response your spouse gave you in return. More likely than not, the response was negative, or at least it was not a fully appreciative response. Usually, when unsolicited advice is given, the receiver will say something like, "I've already tried that," or "No, I don't think that will work."

What spouses need foremost from each other is to be understood, to be heard. It is impossible to overstate the need that each individual has to be listened to and to know that at least one significant person comprehends what is on his or her heart and mind. Solutions have their proper place in communication, but they are not likely to have much punch when they are given before an understanding atmosphere is well established. When answers are given before understanding is established, the listener is likely to interpret one's words as thinly veiled criticism.

With this in mind, you might make attempts to develop reflective listening skills. That is, as your spouse shares feelings with you, show that you comprehend what is being said by summarizing in your own words what you understood your mate to be feeling. For example, a husband who has just been told by his wife that she had a day in which nothing went right might say: "That must have been frustrating. I'll bet you'll be glad when the day is over so you can make a fresh start tomorrow." He would not be giving solutions to his wife's problems, but he would be offering support, so that the wife could then feel strong enough to seek out her own solutions.

Notice a major difference between offering unsolicited solutions and offering understanding. When solutions are doled out, the spouse is covertly suggesting that the mate doesn't have the competence and wisdom to figure out how the problems should be ironed out. But when understanding is given, a compliment is implied as the mate receives the message that his or her feelings are important.

Step 5
Learn to say "You're right"

In the introductory chapter of this book, it was mentioned that some marital discussions tend to resemble a courtroom scene, complete with a prosecutor and a defender. It seems that when sensitive issues arise in marriage, it is easy for mates to square off with each other in a competition to establish who's right and who's wrong.

But of course, when this occurs, the usual outcome of the discussion is that both mates feel defeated.

In a harmonious marriage, spouses *want* to know how the mate perceives matters. There is as strong a desire to know the mate's point of view as there is to pronounce one's own point of view. Harmonious spouses recognize that, in most circumstances, there can be more than one valid perspective and more than one emotional reaction. Therefore, there is a cooperative effort to consider as many aspects of an issue as is possible.

Consequently, when spouses share their thoughts and feelings with each other, there will be a stronger effort to discern what is right about what the mate is saying rather than what is wrong. Harmonious spouses will be willing to acknowledge when the mate has made a good point about an issue. In fact, even when there is not complete agreement, they will still seek areas to agree on.

To illustrate, I recall a wife whose husband had a more liberal attitude about spending money than she did. Throughout the early years of their marriage she would create great arguments by trying to explain to him how foolish he was with his use of money. But she came to realize that, when she did this, her trouble only multiplied.

So in time she learned to use a different approach. Whenever her husband would bring up the subject, for example, of buying a car, she would say something like, "You're right about the fact that we could use some better transportation. It looks like we'll need to consult our budget to see what is feasible." She found that, when she acknowledged his point of view, they were able to rationally discuss the subject at hand and come to an agreeable solution. And to her surprise, she found that when she didn't argue against his point of view he often became more conservative in his plans.

This wife learned that by having an objective approach in arguments, her husband also became more objective and less impulsive. She would feel relieved because she was no longer "the heavy" in their marriage, and he was relieved because he felt that he didn't have to get firm and tough just to prove his power over her.

This practice of saying "You're right" can be implemented in a wide range of circumstances. It can be used when a spouse is expressing hesitancy about recreational plans, or when a spouse points out an error in one's habits, or when discussions arise about childrearing practices. By focusing on points of agreement rather than on points of disagreement, spouses are likely to create a sense of cooperation which can lead to unity in plans.

Step 6
Avoid pleading, convincing, or coaxing

As a corollary to Steps 4 and 5, it can be said that there is little room for arm twisting in harmonious marital communications. One of the most natural human characteristics is the desire to have some sense of independence in one's way of thinking and behaving. As we have discussed several times in this book, the desire for free will was implanted in each individual by God himself. Consequently, it is only natural that most spouses will balk whenever they feel that the mate is imposing an opinion or a behavior on them.

With this in mind, spouses pursuing harmony in marriage will refrain as often as possible from speaking in convincing, pleading, and coaxing overtones. Realizing that these aspects of communication only serve to increase a feeling of opposition, they will attempt instead to communicate in an objective manner. Thoughts and opinions will still be expressed, but they will be done without coercion or insistence.

It is interesting to note that our word *convince* is derived from a Latin root word *vincere* which means to conquer. This implies that, when one individual tries to be

208

convincing in communication with another, there is a distinct attempt on this person's part to gain the upper hand. This automatically means that the other person is on the lower end of the interaction. A game of "one-up, one-down" is then likely to ensue.

So when attempts to convince through communication cease, the couple can expect the communication to be more matter-of-fact in nature. Rather than speaking to one another from an assumed position of superiority, the spouses will be more inclined to speak as co-equals. Spouses will be more likely to use communication in its proper context as an exchange of thoughts and feelings, as opposed to using it to enhance a combative spirit in the home.

Step 7
Set time aside to share personal issues

It is sad to notice how we can easily occupy our time with so many projects that we hardly allow ourselves the luxury of spending time sharing with our mates the things that really matter. Perhaps your house is the kind that is constantly buzzing with activity at virtually all moments of the day. You may have kids noisily running in and out of the house; the washing machine seems to always be on; you have meetings to go to in the evening; and just when you are able to grab a few moments of rest, the phone rings. So guess what gets put on the back shelf? Marital communications.

Whether or not you are the kind of person who seems constantly on the go, you can do yourself a great service by setting aside regular time to spend just with your spouse. This can be done in the latter part of the evening as things begin to quiet down. Or you could choose to eat breakfast together before rushing off to the races. Or regularly you could take time out of your schedule for a pleasant walk around the neighborhood. In addition, regular social outings together (without the kids) can be planned.

The point is that open communication cannot just happen without effort. Since it is so easy to become distracted by any number of outside occurrences, couples who are seeking harmony will structure personal time together. They will check each other's feelings during those times, which will in turn serve to affirm the commitments they have for a successful marriage. They will use the time together to constructively air any needs that might be present. And they will share the occurrences of their days so that there will be a feeling of involvement in each other's lives.

One man told me how he brought new life into his marriage by giving time daily to his wife for the sharing of the events of the day. He said, "When I get home from work each day I spend twenty to thirty minutes talking with my wife about anything that is on our minds. When we do this we both get a super feeling of being close friends. It makes us feel refreshed and enables us to look forward to the rest of the evening, knowing that we are on good footing with each other."

Step 8
When discussing problems, keep their importance in perspective

It is amazing to notice how easy it is to get into emotional blowups over very minor issues. I suppose we all can become red-faced when we think about some of the petty matters that have precipitated great stress in our marriages. Once I talked with a couple who had engaged in a tremendous argument the day prior to seeing me. I learned that the argument had been kicked off by a discussion regarding which pair of socks the husband should wear when they went out to dinner. While they

210

both admitted that the issue was petty, they shared that this kind of confrontation was common in their marriage.

Two problems usually occur that hinder spouses from keeping their disagreements in proper perspective: (a) They let personal feelings like hurt or impatience control them, and (b) They fail to look at how the problem fits into the big picture of life. When spouses let small problems mushroom into big battles, they are allowing themselves to be so caught up in the emotional heat of the moment that rational thinking is lost almost completely.

In order to combat this problem, spouses will benefit by discussing a specific plan that can be used whenever minor issues begin building into major problems. For example, they can agree that, when tensions begin to rise, one of them can call for a thirty-minute "truce" to allow time for the feelings to become settled, thereby making for a higher likelihood that reasonable decisions will be made. Also, they could agree to be more tolerant of each other's quirks and idiosyncracies, which would negate the likelihood of major eruptions taking place.

Couples who are able to keep minor problems in perspective realize that marriage is too important a relationship to allow it to be tarnished by petty gripes and complaints. They have such a strong motivation to live with each other under the umbrella of God's love that they refuse to succumb to the temptation to needle and nit-pick.

Step 9
Look for creative ways to express love

Obviously, the major attraction of marriage is that it is a relationship that offers each spouse the hope of being loved and accepted. In Chapter 12 we discussed how God chose to give us life for the sake of coming into contact with his love. And we noted that God designed marital relations for the purpose of allowing us the opportunity to know love in the human arena, which would in turn help us to conceptualize love in the spiritual arena. There is no greater privilege on earth than to become involved in a relationship in which God's plan for love can be enacted.

When couples first fall in love they rarely have difficulty in feeling motivated to express it. Acts of kindness are common, long discussions are held, physical touching is evident, as well as times of romantic embrace. But when the thrill of the new relationship wears off, many of these once-exuberant couples find it difficult to express their love. A certain stiffness may come to their manifestations of love because extraneous factors (busy schedules, children, disagreements) hinder its expression.

It's not that these couples lose the ability to show love. Not at all. Rather, the problem is that these couples can lose sight of the need for creativity in the giving of love. Signs of this stiffness in giving love may include strained communication, lowered sexual interests, difficulty in sharing personal feelings, and an absence of warm touching.

Consequently, in order to keep the embers of love glowing, it would be to a couple's advantage to think of the various ways love can be expressed. The manifestations of love can be obvious, such as giving hugs, expressing love verbally, or sitting together while spending time at home in the evenings. Or the manifestations of love may take on more subtle forms, such as asking questions about a subject of interest to the spouse, doing unsolicited favors for each other, or going out of one's way to act kindly while doing mundane household chores.

Love is a feeling, but love is also a plan of action. It involves the heart, but it also involves one's attitude and behaviors. This means that, even if high sentimental feelings toward one's mate are not always present, love can still be expressed. The key for a sustained atmosphere of love in the home is that the spouses are aware of varied ways to keep the love alive in routine matters.

With this in mind, ask yourself the following questions:

How do I tend to communicate my love to my spouse?

What specific behaviors please my spouse the most?

Do I touch my spouse regularly, indicating a gentleness toward him or her?

When I am home with my spouse do I think often about my partner's need to know of my love?

What pleasant behavior could I show my spouse that would come as a complete and refreshing surprise?

Step 10
Live with your spouse as unto the Lord

This final step in our formula for harmonious living is the most important one. It implies that we each will see our mates as such valuable individuals that we will offer them the same respect we would offer if we were tangibly interacting with God himself. While it may be impossible to do this with perfect consistency, it is a worthy goal to aim at.

Just before being delivered for crucifixion, Jesus Christ told his disciples, "Just as the Father has loved me, I have also loved you; abide in My love" (John 15:9). When he spoke these words, Jesus was at the end of a three-year period of time in which he had constantly demonstrated his love and regard for his select disciples. As his earthly mission was about to culminate in his victory over sin, he reminded his disciples to continue living in the love that they had learned in their interactions with him.

Just as the disciples were instructed to interact with others in the love of Jesus Christ, so are marriage partners to interact with each other. When each mate comes to have a saving knowledge of the love of God, the desire of that person's heart will be to seize every opportunity to illustrate to the mate one's devotion to a Spirit-led style of life. The Christian spouse knows that, as the characteristics of love (joy, patience, kindness) are evidenced in one's marriage, the Lord is pleased. By loving one's mate, one is paying homage and devotion to God.

As mentioned earlier, it is easy to specify some of the how-to steps that are a part of harmonious marital communication. But it is difficult to maintain the high amount of concentration involved in developing positive communications into a habitual way of life. You will succeed in making this formula work for you in direct proportion to your effort to place Christian principles into the heart of your marital interactions.

15

Taking the Initiative

A woman once shared with me that she was a walking encyclopedia of psychological information. She said she could recite all sorts of psychological theories of personalities and formulas for successful living. Yet she still had a hard time following through with her insights. She told me, "I've read so many self-improvement books that I could easily write my own best seller. But my life is still in shambles. What am I going to do?" Her inability to move from information gathering to practical application was rendering her knowledge useless.

Many people have found themselves in this same frustrating position of knowing what to do with their lives, yet failing to get the job done. These people may be the type who are temporarily motivated by a good book or a lively pep talk, yet eventually find themselves falling back into the same habits that dogged them before. Why is this? What causes us to fall short of our goals even when we know what to do?

By nature most of us tend to be impatient in problem-solving. In fact, our high-tech, quick-fix, late-twentieth-century mentality is such that we expect problems to go away as quickly as we can push a button. Through experience, we have been taught to find fast and easy solutions to the broadest array of problems. Think about some of the common, easy solutions we customarily call upon when various troubles arise.

> If we get a headache, we can simply swallow a couple of aspirin tablets , and in a few short minutes it is gone.

> When the car breaks down, we call a wrecker and let the man at the service station fix it. (And we fuss at him if he is too slow!)

> When we are hungry, we scoot around to a fast-food restaurant for a ready-made meal.

> If the temperature is too warm, we flip on the air conditioner. When it is cold, we turn up the heat.

> When our socks have holes in them, we simply throw them away and buy new ones.

We have come to expect simple solutions for virtually any problem. If we would compare our quick-fix mentality to the work ethic of five or six generations ago, we would conclude that motivation to work out our problems by the sweat of our brows has decreased dramatically with each passing generation.

Naturally, if we have this quick-fix mentality toward the trivial problems in our everyday lives, we can expect a spill-over effect into our desire and motivation to "sweat out" our problems in psychological and relationship areas. Since we live in a culture that tends to expect (even demand) convenience, it is quite predictable that we would hold the same mentality in solving the most personal of problems. When difficulties arise in our homes, our natural tendency instinctively is to wish so hard for an instant cure that we lose the motivation to be patiently deliberate in making the gains and positive changes we so deeply desire.

Case Example

Charles admitted openly that his greatest problem was his impatience, particularly as it was displayed toward his wife and kids. He was a highly knowledgeable man with firm principles, but he just couldn't bring himself to the point of accepting the fact that there were times when things at home just wouldn't go according to his set ways. He explained it this way: "When I'm at work, I know that things will go right, because I'm in full command of my area. My employees know that if they don't perform well, they can be fired. And I also know that if a machine breaks down and quits functioning, we can replace it at the snap of a finger. Everything in my office is set up so that it will cater to me. Maybe that's why I have a hard time at home with my wife and kids. They don't 'jump to' like mechanical gadgets. They each have a mind of their own." Indeed, Charles was correct in his self-analysis. He was so accustomed to having things fall conveniently into place that he was not mentally prepared to grind it out at home.

While it is pleasurable to live in a lifestyle that offers easy solutions to various mechanical inconveniences, we must remind ourselves that relationships are not necessarily subject to the same quick-fix approach. It takes both time and effort to create an atmosphere of satisfaction in any relationship, particularly marriage. We must set aside our craving for instant solutions in our differences and mentally prepare for a sustained level of effort in our communication practices.

With this in mind, let's compare two kinds of attitudes that can be seen as couples make the effort to bring harmony into their home. One of these attitudes is not likely to be successful, while the other is. As you examine these two attitudes, keep in mind that you can choose for yourself which way you will go.

Passive Attitudes Versus Committed Attitudes

When we are constantly exposed to convenience as a

way of life, it is very easy to develop a mindset of passivity. That is, we can learn to sit back and let problems take care of themselves while we expend a minimal amount of effort. In a marriage relationship, this might mean that one or both spouses will dream of having a picture-perfect union, but little will be done on a consistent basis to bring it about. For example, a couple might say to themselves, "We ought to have more love expressed in our home," but then do little to actually make it happen. Notice some of the common attitudes held by individuals who are prone to the passive way of relating.

Passive Attitudes

What are you going to do about our problems? Typically, a person with the passive attitude tends to think first and foremost about what one's spouse should be doing when there are problems. True to the quick-fix mentality, this individual will look outside of self for problem resolution.

What's in it for me? Along the same lines, passive individuals tend to think in terms of what they will receive from the partner (as opposed to what they will give). Their minds tend to focus more quickly on what their spouse can do to please them.

I'll try if you will. When passive individuals finally do get around to thinking about the ways they can help the marriage, there is usually a stipulation attached. Their efforts are almost entirely dependent on the fact that the spouse is going to be working right alongside them. If the spouse is not in the frame of mind to make marital improvements, passive people will say, "Forget it. It's not worth the trouble." All good intentions are quickly dropped.

Maybe in time things will get better. Passive individuals are forever looking for excuses to postpone the efforts involved in making relationships work. Consequently, they frequently latch onto the idea that time cures all ills.

While there is some truth to the fact that time can heal wounds, there is nothing magic about time. By depending on the passing of days to solve problems, these individuals are attempting to absolve self of the effort of work.

It's just not fair! When it becomes apparent to passive individuals how much work will be involved in the marriage relationship, they throw their hands into the air with a cry of "unfair!" And particularly when the spouse doesn't seem to be putting out much effort, they cry out all the more. They let the issue of fairness determine whether or not efforts to improve will be made.

As you can easily determine, the passive mind-set does little to help couples make the necessary efforts to ensure success in marriage. To the contrary, this attitude only increases the likelihood of frustration and repeated defensiveness.

Let's contrast this with a mind-set that encourages the individual to be an initiator.

Committed Attitudes

I'm in it all the way. When a spouse develops an attitude of commitment toward marriage, there is a deep and abiding desire to see the relationship through to the end. This person recognizes that the marriage commitment is parallel to God's undying commitment to his church. So in an effort to imitate God, every effort is made to make the relationship one that will last.

What can I do for you? Rather than being one who wishes to be served, the committed spouse is one who looks for ways to be the servant. There is an acknowledgment of the biblical teaching that says "It is more blessed to give than to receive" (Acts 20:35).

I'll do it, rather than I'll try. When a spouse takes an attitude of commitment there is no question about that person's intentions. This person makes it very clear to self and to others that an effort definitely will be made to the fullest measure of one's capacity. Rather than saying "I'll try to do better" (which often implies that the effort may be less than complete), the committed person is definitive when plans are laid out. He will say, instead, "I'll do it; you can count on me."

Fairness is not the ultimate issue. When one spouse makes a concerted effort to be the very best spouse he or she knows how to be, there is a high likelihood that, at some point, an observation could be made that the other spouse isn't working as hard in the marriage. But when this occurs, the committed spouse is not one to become sidetracked by the issue of fairness. This person knows that if arguments erupt over what is fair and what is not fair, the marriage will lose ground. Consequently, the determination is made to continue in one's efforts even if the work is not always split fifty-fifty.

Marital Commitment: An Extension of One's Relationship with God

Almost inevitably, a spouse's commitment to marriage will be strengthened as his or her relationship with God grows, since the very nature of God is permeated with qualities like love, peace, and gentleness. In addition, God has shown himself to be a relentless pursuer who will not weaken in his efforts to illustrate his love to the ones he has created. So as a spouse becomes closely acquainted with God's attributes, these qualities are bound to become more and more prominent in that person. The net result will be that the individual will more likely exhibit God-like qualities in relationships, particularly in marriage.

James 4:8 tells us, "Draw near to God and he will draw near to you." This verse implies that as our commitment to him grows so also does our ability to live in his ways. But the crucial question to be asked is this, "How can I effectively draw near to God?"

220

Let's examine several ways to draw near to God.

Have an active prayer life. Prayer is not something that is done simply before meals or at bedtime with the kids. Prayer is an activity that can be pursued at any time of the day or night. In fact, 1 Thessalonians 5:17 exhorts us to "pray without ceasing." That is, in our daily routines we can each strive to have a conscious awareness of the presence and guidance of God. We can converse with him in both the mundane decisions of the day and in the crucial ones. We can concentrate on his instructions as we learn to control our emotions and our communications.

We must remind ourselves that God does not instruct us to pray just so he might have an opportunity to hear us voice our needs and opinions. He already knows those things before we do! Rather, God instructs us to pray because it is a means for us to maintain contact with him and with his will for our lives. Through an active prayer life we mentally dwell on our need for his strength and direction. In other words, prayer isn't something that God needs, prayer is something that we need to keep us close to him.

Live in the knowledge of God's presence in your life. Before ascending to heaven after his resurrection from the dead, Jesus Christ gave an assurance to all his disciples when he said, "And lo, I am with you always, even to the end of the age" (Matt. 28:20). Though he is not currently with his family in body, he is ever with us in his Holy Spirit. This means that we are never alone. We are never without him as our divine companion. And when we recognize his status of being present everywhere, we can then derive a motivation to live exactly as if he were standing next to us.

Think of the implications this would have in our marriages. If spouses would live in the awareness of being in the presence of God himself, we would be far more conscientious in the words we speak and in the moods we project. As an example, when you have special company in your house for dinner, you are probably more likely to be polite and courteous to your mate. So it can be when we live in the knowledge of God's presence. Our behavior will become more even-keeled and our moods more temperate.

Have a regular group communion with God. To have communion with God means that we will participate in a fellowship experience with him. This can be accomplished by banding together with a local group of Christians in a worship center, and it can be accomplished by having regular times of family devotion in one's home. By joining in worshipful experiences with family members and with fellow believers, we are drawn collectively into the power and presence of God. When we do this, there is bound to be a spill-over effect in the way we commune directly with our mates.

Desire to show God's love to others. Nothing pleases God more than to see his followers giving his love to others. First John 4:21 tells us, "And this commandment we have from Him, that the one who loves God should love his brother also." It is by demonstrating our love to others that we illustrate our commitment to God, because God is love. And we show that we know his love by imitating it as often as possible.

As you examine the various ways that one's personal commitment to God can be displayed, you will readily determine that the individual who comes to the point of deep commitment to him will also experience a deep level of commitment in one's marriage relationship. It is virtually impossible to be committed to God while having a disdain for human relationships. As we grow in our loyalty to him, so do we grow in all other relations.

Case Example

Dean shared with me how he had once lived a free-wheeling lifestyle in which the only person that really mattered to him was himself. He was married during this time, but he would be the first to admit that his wife suffered substantially from depression because of his poor treatment of her and his unpredictable ways. He was often sharp in his speaking style, he was regularly on edge in his moods, and he was quite rebellious in his social habits (drinking heavily and staying out late).

Just when Dean and his wife were at the point of divorce, he was approached by a friend who began talking with him about his need to make a commitment to give his life to God. Dean had been to church before and he was familiar with the notion of living for the Lord. But he never truly considered it as something he needed to do. But since his life was such a wreck and his family life was in shambles, he decided that he would look into the matter.

As Dean explored what it meant to make a commitment to God, he realized that it didn't mean that he would become bound to just follow an endless list of dos and don'ts. Rather, he learned that a commitment to God through his Son, Jesus Christ, meant that he would be able to live with such traits as love, gentleness, and forgiveness. He understood that such a lifestyle would be the beginning step toward finding the satisfaction that he had always longed for. With his friend, Dean prayed that Jesus would come into his heart and give him a new life.

Upon giving his life to Christ, Dean found that his old attitudes and feelings began to change. For example, he no longer had the yearning for a rebellious lifestyle of living a wild "night life." His anger and irritable moods decreased, giving way instead to softness and kindness. Rather than being preoccupied with himself, he became preoccupied with showing his wife, family, and friends the love that he had found in his relationship with God. He even began going to church and to lead Bible studies at home with his wife. His entire perspective on living changed! Dean very boldly points to the day that he made a commitment to live for God as the day his life turned around.

Because a commitment to God teaches an individual to understand that life has been designed for relationships, the relationship that stands the most to gain is one's marriage. When God is in control of a husband-wife team, they will find the necessary ways to openly share their love. The need for defensiveness will be replaced by a desire to build each other up. Commitment to the task is not a problem in this case.

223

Self-Adequacy: The Core Ingredient

Earlier, in chapter 5, it was mentioned that a major factor in defensive communication is a fragile ego. So it is only natural to assume that if a person is to make the appropriate changes to ensure a pattern of harmony, the opposite trait will be needed—a sense of self-adequacy.

It is difficult, even impossible, for a mate to make proper commitments in marriage without a strong foundation for inner stability. Since our outward behaviors are a direct manifestation of our inner beliefs, feelings, and attitudes, it is logical to assume that stable communications come from stable inner ingredients. A house will not stand without a solid foundation, and neither will our abilities to relate properly.

So how does an individual come to the point of having that stable inner foundation of self-adequacy? It comes by knowing God's love for each individual. And it comes by acknowledging the worth and value given to each by the Creator. In Romans 8:31, the apostle Paul asked the rhetorical question, "If God is for us, who is against us?" By that he was indicating that there is no power on earth that can negate the fact that God's love is far deeper and more comprehensive than we can ever imagine.

When we hold firmly to the notion of our adequacy and value in Christ, we have the necessary core ingredient to defeat pesky defensiveness, opting instead for the more rewarding life of harmony. We can take the initiative of letting ourselves be fully known, of being open in sharing God-like traits, and in communicating in an encouraging fashion, because we know that God will supply us with the tools needed to accomplish success in our marriage.

By fixing our minds on his Word, we can allow him to live in us and through us. That fact is a certainty. As we do this, we will find that we are fully prepared to overcome the temptation to just sit back and let the marriage "flow its course." Rather, we will exhibit the consistency and concentration that comes from knowing that we are adequate to the task of becoming harmonizers.

224